Implementing Ethics in E
Ethnography

Providing theoretical grounding, case studies and practical solutions, *Implementing Ethics in Educational Ethnography* examines how researchers can overcome ethical dilemmas associated with and encountered during ethnographic research. From the initial stages of research design such as consideration from regulatory bodies, through research occurring in the field to project completion and reporting, it explores many of the factors associated with ensuring culturally sensitive and ethical studies.

The book covers key questions including:

- What can researchers expect of ethical review boards?
- Where and with whom should dialogue take place about ethicality within research?
- What effect does a research focus have on regulation and research practice?
- What is the effect of context on ethical practices?
- Does the positionality of a researcher have an effect on ethical practices?
- How do we ensure that ethicality supports the trustworthiness of research projects?

Using a range of international case studies, *Implementing Ethics in Educational Ethnography* provides researchers and students with invaluable details about how to navigate the field, ensuring that they can sustain good ethical practice throughout the life of a research project.

Hugh Busher is an Honorary Associate Professor in the School of Education at the University of Leicester, UK.

Alison Fox is a Senior Lecturer at the Faculty of Wellbeing, Education and Language Studies at the Open University, UK.

Implementing Ethics in Educational Ethnography

Regulation and Practice

Edited By Hugh Busher and Alison Fox

Routledge
Taylor & Francis Group
LONDON AND NEW YORK

First published 2019
by Routledge
2 Park Square, Milton Park, Abingdon, Oxon, OX14 4RN

and by Routledge
52 Vanderbilt Avenue, New York, NY 10017

Routledge is an imprint of the Taylor & Francis Group, an informa business

British Library Cataloguing-in-Publication Data
A catalogue record for this book is available from the British Library

Library of Congress Cataloging-in-Publication Data
Names: Busher, Hugh, editor. | Fox, Alison, editor.
Title: Implementing ethics in educational ethnography : regulation and practice /
    edited by Hugh Busher and Alison Fox.
Description: Abingdon, Oxon ; New York, NY : Routledge, 2019. | Includes
    bibliographical references.
Identifiers: LCCN 2018055751| ISBN 9781138580237 (hbk) |
    ISBN 9781138580251 (pbk) | ISBN 9780429507489 (ebk)
Subjects: LCSH: Educational anthropology—Methodology. |
    Education—Research—Moral and ethical aspects. | Anthropological ethics.
Classification: LCC LB45 .I48 2019 | DDC 306.43—dc23
LC record available at https://lccn.loc.gov/2018055751

ISBN: 978-1-138-58023-7 (hbk)
ISBN: 978-1-138-58025-1 (pbk)
ISBN: 978-0-429-50748-9 (ebk)

Typeset in Galliard
by Swales & Willis Ltd, Exeter, Devon, UK
Printed by CPI Group (UK) Ltd, Croydon CR0 4YY

Contents

Contributors

Begoña Vigo Arrazola is Associate Professor in the Department of Didactics and School Organization at the Faculty of Education, University of Zaragoza, Spain.

Dennis Beach is Professor of Education in the Department of Education and Education Research, University of Borås, and Professor in the Department of Education and Special Education, University of Gothenburg, Sweden.

Hugh Busher is an Honorary Associate Professor in the School of Education at the University of Leicester, UK.

Barbara Dennis is Associate Professor of Inquiry Methodology at Indiana University, USA.

Marianne Dovemark is Professor in Education at the Faculty of Education and Special Education, University of Gothenburg, Sweden.

Alison Fox is a Senior Lecturer at the Faculty of Wellbeing, Education and Language Studies at the Open University, UK.

Rafael Mitchell is Lecturer at the School of Education, University of Bristol, UK and Research Associate at the Faculty of Education, University of Cambridge, UK.

Hanna M. Nikkanen is Postdoctoral Researcher in the Sibelius Academy at the University of the Arts Helsinki, Finland.

Sofia Marques da Silva is Assistant Professor at the Faculty of Psychology and Education Sciences, University of Porto, Portugal.

Ingrid Smette is Senior Researcher at Norwegian Social Research, Oslo Metropolitan University, Norway.

Anna Traianou is Reader in Educational Studies in the Department of Educational Studies at Goldsmiths, University of London, UK.

Foreword

Sofia Marques da Silva

I remember well when, in 2006, I was exposed to a contentious situation while doing fieldwork in a youth centre. I would write about this seven years later, but at the time I experienced a negotiation process, with glimpses of naivety, with participants and myself, in order to defend ethical principles that would go beyond or against standard ethical codes. Since then, ethnographers have become acquainted with new research resources and tools, have followed participants and phenomena in new contexts and have been dealing with old, but also with emerging or amplified, ethical challenges.

The idea behind this book is to provide researchers in education, and other social sciences doing ethnography, or engaged in other qualitative research methods, with situated knowledge on how ethnographers are reacting, reflecting and developing new understandings and solutions for concrete ethical dilemmas.

The chapters assembled in this volume have been written by a collection of experts engaged in doing ethnography in the field of education. Altogether, they offer an invaluable contribution to a wider understanding of different research ethical challenges by debating analytical dimensions and approaches that often we find disjointed, and by reporting experiences without the attempt to reach definite judgements. Through this book we may envisage possibilities to redefine procedures and recommendations for ethnographic research, while preserving research integrity and the protection of participants' interests and rights.

Chapters in this book deliberate on research ethics' key questions and consider the problems in many ethical topics, such as: emerging dangerous situations regarding the loss of researchers' autonomy and research through over-control by research institutions; the dilemma of ethnography being affected by new procedures of monitoring research ethics while engaging vulnerable populations in the research process; and the impact of changes in methodological teaching and learning among emerging researchers. Some chapters address ethical challenges that may be considered more specific to ethnography, such as those coming from doing research in open spaces or the impossibility to anticipate some ethical risks in order to be included in the protocol for ethical review boards. How may an ethnographer predict the impact of her/his presence, particularly when familiarity exists with a given context? Considering the context of ethnographic research, the relationship between the researcher and participants is often mediated by a set of specific and complex confidentiality engagements and commitments. Sometimes, as is also advanced in this book, relationships are developed beyond those of informed consent at the start of a project.

Some years ago, Tolich and Fitzgerald (2006) discussed, analysed and presented alternatives to ethics review processes designed for qualitative research by writing a piece that they entitled "If ethics committees were designed for ethnography". These authors concluded that if it is accepted that research, and unquestionably ethnographic research, is always situated, review boards might radically reimagine their role such that the researcher becomes viewed as the expert and the board as the learner in terms of learning about ethnography. This will involve a process of negotiation including different identities, subjectivities, power relations, mutual exploitation and positionalities. How do researchers convince ethics committees that this is part of ethnography and still ethically rigorous? How do we balance convictions and conventions with the need to keep public trust in our research?

The issue of standardisation of research processes, often through the blind application of standard regulations, frequently done by ethics committees unfamiliar with ethnography, needs to be accompanied by a critical reflection. This should involve all researchers in reviewing what constitute comprehensive and situated guidelines for responsible conduct and the effectiveness of standard procedures in education research quality and its impact in ethnography.

Issues of ethics, research regulation and ethics boards are part of contemporary institutions of higher education, but they might imply the need to deal with sets of hurdles among researchers willing to undertake ethnography. Many ethnographers' contexts are situated in vulnerable contexts and they often find themselves at a crossroads of responding to different ethical requests. As pointed out in this book, these tensions may appear at any point during the life of the project – from the design to the dissemination. If senior or emerging ethnographers feel that they may face the impossibility of combining the doings of such ethnographic work with seeking research approval, they are likely to be discouraged.

The danger of blind regulation, no matter what methods or topics people are researching, can cause more harm than good and end up in researchers avoiding controversial contexts, investing in "neutral areas" or in hiding their positioning.

The rigidity, pressure or the mandatory procedures to follow medical models' regulations (as presented in this book as the basis for traditional review board and national protocols and guidance) in order to validate ethnographic research might limit the research topics chosen. With so many constraints in doing qualitative and ethnographic research, researchers may end up "choosing" easily researchable topics, using fast methods, that will provide the researcher more quickly with results that are analytically less complex but might be better organised into simple results that can be used more easily by politicians. The effort that is invested will have a faster and more visible turnout at public level.

It was in the context of Network 19 Ethnography, during the 2017 conference of the European Educational Research Association (EERA), that symposia led by Hugh Busher and Alison Fox, editors of the present work and distinguished scholars, grounded and inspired the organisation of this volume. Over the years, since its beginning in 1999, Network 19 welcomed and activated discussions on ethical procedures and challenges while doing ethnography in education. This book also represents part of the network memory and patrimony. For this accomplishment, I would like to congratulate and acknowledge the editors and all contributors.

The book represents, for me as researcher, but particularly as a research methodology teacher and a supervisor, a fundamental asset and, therefore, I don't hesitate in highly recommending it.

Reference

Tolich, M. & Fitzgerald, M. H. (2006). If Ethics Committees Were Designed for Ethnography. *Journal of Empirical Research on Human Research Ethics*, 1(2), 71–78. https://doi.org/10.1525/jer.2006.1.2.71.

Chapter 1

Introduction

Overview of the book

Hugh Busher and Alison Fox

Introduction

At present many books on research methods focus on the theory of ethics and how to apply it when starting a research project, but there is relatively little discussion on applying research ethics in practice throughout the life of a qualitative research project and the importance of researcher reflexivity to that process. This book focuses on the practice of ethics and how ethical practice can be sustained by researchers in the field throughout the life of research projects using ethnographic and other qualitative approaches to research.

The extension of ethical regulation over the past twenty years from medicine and psychology across the whole of social science has made it more difficult for researchers to explain why ethnographic research in education needs to be carried out in certain ways that often differ from those of medicine and the physical sciences while still being ethically sound. Ethical regulation is largely carried out by research ethics committees, known in some countries as institutional (ethical) review boards, which decide if research projects can be implemented, and on what terms. Other countries, particularly in Scandinavia, have central or national review bodies to support researchers in their ethical thinking and to police their practice.

This regulatory regime has posed problems for ethnographic and other qualitative research because it is based on a medical and physical science model of enquiry. Not least, it pre-supposes levels of potential harm to participants arising from invasive and other physical processes that are highly unlikely ever to occur in qualitative research. However, it is not unreasonable for participants, gatekeepers and beneficiaries of research to wish to be sure that researchers have taken care to act in manners that are intended to prevent harm to participants in, and the environment of, a research project. It has led to a public demand that researchers show that they can sustain auditable ethical practices. Nonetheless, the formal regulatory procedures have introduced significant delays into the inception of research projects, as well as raising questions about the validity of some research designs that are needed for studying human interaction in certain situations. Some researchers have even argued that the new regulatory regime is an infringement of academic freedom to pursue research deemed necessary for understanding social and political processes in society.

The main gatekeepers to whether or not a study is approved to proceed are variously called research ethics committees (RECs) or institutional review boards (IRBs), seemingly depending on which side of the Atlantic you live. Both terms are used in the chapters in this book. They are usually convened by academic institutions to police the quality of research projects proposed by researchers and to ensure the proposed projects meet the ethical protocols supported by an institution and the relevant ethical guidance or codes of conduct of the professional body or bodies in the researcher's field, and to give researchers confidence that they have the support of their organisation in their work. However, in some Scandinavian countries RECs are not institutionally based but government-based, as some of the chapters in this book illustrate. In addition, researchers might also have to pass their projects through ethical review if their studies are undertaken with funding from sponsors, including government ministries, or in specific research settings, such as within healthcare or prison service settings.

Ethnographic enquiry proposals often face particular challenges when being considered by IRBs as some board members are often unfamiliar with the methodology and how its data collection processes need to be provisional at the beginning of a project. Even if board support is granted based on an agreed set of practices about entry to the field and securing informed consent from potential participants, this does not always help ethnographers as they confront methodological dilemmas in the field (Rashid, Cain & Goez 2015). Once in the field, relationships develop in ways not easy to anticipate and data emerge that are of interest beyond those accessible through initial informed consent to participate in research. This places particular responsibilities on the ethnographer through significant self-reflection on ethical practice (Fine 1993) and also trust in the researcher from the institution.

This book discusses how researchers can carry out ethical educational ethnographic research in a variety of face-to-face public educational spaces, as well as in online and hybrid spaces. This includes researchers persuading organs of research supervision, such as ethical review boards, as well as stakeholders and participants in research projects that they will carry out their research in an ethical manner throughout the life of a research project and afterwards, during its publication phase. It also addresses the dilemmas of people carrying out research in happenstance situations when it might not be clear from whom to gain consent to carry out research, either at the beginning of a project or during the life of a project as the research process develops through time. Yet not gaining this permission raises questions about how responsibly a researcher is behaving.

Contributions to the book focus on how researchers can construct and apply knowledge of ethical practice to ethnographic studies in different educational situations to make clear to putative participants in and gatekeepers of their proposed research projects that these will be carried out in an ethical manner.

It also focuses on the dilemmas in the field that educational researchers encounter when trying to enact ethical practice and how they might resolve these. It is intended that this book helps researchers in the field to cope wisely with the ethical dilemmas that they may encounter while also helping ethical regulatory bodies at national and institutional levels to come to wise decisions when faced with research applications that may challenge tightly constructed notions of what constitutes ethical research practice.

Different ethical frameworks/approaches to ethical practice

Ethical decision-making can be considered to operate at five levels (Kitchener & Kitchener 2009), each of which are problematised in chapters in this book.

The first level is related to a researcher's ethical decision-making in their own research setting through an analysis of the research scenario and their responses. This level is illustrated in this book through different researchers' perspectives both culturally and personally: Nikkanen's chapter about her role as a teacher and researcher in a Finnish school (Chapter 6); Smette's chapter (Chapter 4) and that of Fox and Mitchell (Chapter 8) about the experiences of undertaking ethnographic study of schools in Norway and Ethiopia, respectively; Dovemark's chapter about the ethical dilemmas faced in studying public recruitment fairs of Swedish schools (Chapter 7). A key argument presented throughout the book is how demanding such decision-making is for ethnographers and in particular how, if researchers are to ethically meet the needs of those they research, entering only with pre-determined ways of behaving underpinned by agreed principles and practices will be insufficient. Decision-making, as for all social science research but argued in this book as a particular concern in ethnographic studies, needs to continue into the fieldwork and reporting phases. This book's chapters therefore explore how both researcher and regulatory practices need to support researchers in being able to be responsive to their fieldwork experiences to ensure culturally sensitive and ethical studies.

The second level of ethical decision-making refers to the ethical rules bound up in professional codes of practice, ethical guidance and legislative regulations. Such codes and guidance are constructed for the membership of particular professions such as national psychological and sociological associations, broader educational and social science research associations, such as the American Educational Research Association, the UK Academy of Social Science and the British Educational Research Association, as well as formal national bodies that regulate research, e.g., the Economic Social Research Council (UK) and ministries, such as those in Sweden, Finland and Norway. Such guidance is set within a broader legislative landscape relating to issues such as data protection, criminal disclosure and child protection. The codes provide guidance which explain researchers' legal obligations when carrying out research and need to keep up-to-date with legislative changes.

In Europe, 2018 saw a major launch of new data protection regulation with the General Data Protection Regulation (2018), which affects all those collecting, processing and storing data in the European Union as well as transferring data in and out of the EU and to which national data protection acts have responded with amendments, e.g., the UK Data Protection Act (2018). Institutions within which research is carried out, as well as funding bodies such as research councils (e.g., the National Health and Medical Research Council, Research Council and Vice Chancellors' Committee in Australia) and national ministries who create ethical codes of practice for their researchers. Together this leads to a web of codified rules that a single researcher needs to navigate and, where the codes appear contradictory, make decisions. The codes are usually regulated by associated review processes ultimately overseen by RECs or IRBs as referred to earlier in this chapter. It is notable that none of these codes are written with any specific methodology in mind and further work is needed by researchers in holding up the various advice they are beholden to against the values associated with their chosen research approach. For ethnographers, this "mean(s) our personal sense of ethics and our ethnographic sense of ethics are not separate from one another" (Dennis 2018: 53). Busher's chapter in this book (Chapter 5), for example, explores the thinking, rules and practical applicability of the concept of vulnerable participants in the context of educational ethnography.

Above the level of codified rules sits a third level of ethical decision-making, that of ethical principles. These underpin the second level to provide a justification for the advice and hence guide first-level decision-making. However, if we look across such guidance internationally there can be seen to be both agreement and difference in the priorities given to the key underpinning principles (see Table 1.1).

In terms of overlap, respect for persons (to be shown in a number of ways), beneficience and non-maleficence (balancing the maximising of benefits against the minimisation of harm), research integrity and accountability feature as common concerns across the most recent versions of these codes. There has been a shift over time as such national sets of principles have been reviewed from their origins in biomedical research. Whilst respect for persons and beneficience can be traced back even before the Belmont report (DHEW 1979) to the Nuremberg Code (1947) and the Declaration of Helsinki (WMA 1964, 2013), the latter two principles of accountability and research integrity have moved into the language of regulation and hence become increasingly explicit in more recent updates. The phenomenon of increasing expectations of researchers to make a social impact has been noted as a modern concern at the regulatory level and one that brings its own challenges in terms of defining and prioritising this against other principles (Mustajoki & Mustajoki 2017). This pushes funding towards applied research, particularly in the case of development aid funding. This could lead to a limitation of what is considered valid research if only simple 'what works' studies are funded rather than research that both quests for fundamental understanding and consideration of its use (Wiliam 2011).

Table 1.1 Principles in selected ethical research guidelines

Principles	Guidelines								
	1	2	3	4	5	6	7	8	9
a Respect for persons	*	*	* key	*	* key	*	* key	* key	
b Beneficence and non-maleficence	*	*	*				*	*	
c Justice	*	*	*	*					
d Research merit and integrity		*			*	* key	*	*	
e Honesty						*			*
f Concern for welfare/duty of care				*					
g Fairness			* key						* key
h Responsibility for future generations									* key
i Accountability					* key	*	* key	* key	*
j Inclusivity (of interests, values, funders, methods and perspectives)							*		
k Professional competence					*				
l Independence of researcher								*	
m Voluntary and informed consent								*	

Source: Table largely based on Kitty de Riele (Brooks, de Riele & Maguire 2014: 30–31)

Key

1 **DHEW, 'The Belmont Report' – 1979 (USA)**
2 **NHMRC, ARC and AVCC – 2007; updated 2018 (Australia)**
3 **CNdeS –2012 (Brazil)**

   a *(autonomy)*; g. *(equity)*

4 **CIHR, NSERC and SSHRC – 2010 (Canada)**
5. **AERA – 2011 (US)**

   a *(for rights, dignity and diversity)*;
   i *(professional, scientific, scholarly and social responsibility)*

6 **ALLEA – 2017 (Europe)**

   d *(reliability)*

7 **BERA and AcSS – 2018 and 2015 (UK)**

   a *(for privacy, autonomy, diversity, values and dignity)*;
   i *(social responsibilities for conducting and disseminating)*

8. **ESRC – 2010; updated 2018 (UK)**

   a *(for rights and dignity)*; i. *(accountability and transparency)*

9 **World Conference on Research Integrity: Singapore Statement – 2010**

   g *(and professional courtesy)*; h. *(good stewardship on behalf of others)*

Two of the codes feature integrity in their titles (ALLEA 2017; World Conference on Research Integrity 2010). These, and the other codes which prioritise the principle of integrity, link the quality of research explicitly with ethical considerations and place responsibilities on researchers to be transparent about their research designs and conduct. This links with the increased expectations of accountability. On the other hand, justice, one of the three common principles adopted from the earlier biomedical codes (Israel 2015) is less universally represented as a key principle in those reviewed (Table 1.1). This may be as social science ethical guidelines seek to take a more proactive approach to ethical guidance than the earlier agreements, which were often created as a reactive response to malpractice. However, this coming of age in social science-specific guidance is being challenged to ensure that the "'bottom-up' discipline and institutionally sensitive approaches" being replaced by "'top-down' more centralized approaches" (Israel 2015: 77) does not drift towards risk averseness, rather than fully representing the concerns of participants in social science studies. As can be seen from Table 1.1, relational concerns as a duty of care can be seen only to feature at a principled level in Canadian ethical guidance.

There have been nations that have tried to be inclusive of all groups of society in generating their ethical regulation, such as the approach in Brazil to include its indigenous populations (CNdeS 2012). However, this has been difficult to enact and has been accused in practice of limiting research with such communities (Israel 2015). In part the issues arising from this approach have been related to applying Western principles of individual autonomy, rather than accepting local conceptions of, for example, social and community assent, and in part to do with the positivist underpinnings of the regulatory codes. These issues lead to social science researchers in many contexts needing to apply waivers in the application of the positivist ethical protocols and hence being seen as non-normative. Inclusivity of methodologies is still something which is not accepted in all national contexts. Interestingly inclusivity in its broadest sense has been prioritised in recently launched UK ethical guidance by the Academy of Social Sciences (2015), then adopted by the British Educational Research Association (2018). This book challenges and offers empirically based advice as to how the full range of ethnographic approaches might be reviewed and deemed acceptable by regulatory bodies and hence ethnographers feel empowered to prepare and defend their work to gain institutional and funder support.

It is noteworthy that there are some national contexts that have no ethical guidance to support researchers, particularly across the African continent. In these and similar contexts such as Pakistan any advice is usually limited to bioethical principles, with seemingly little national (political) appetite for developing social science-specific advice. Where such guidance exists, it is usually imported from Western contexts, rather than being locally derived or adapted to ensure it is culturally sensitive (Chilisa 2009; Qureshi 2011). Difficulties in applying Western expectations, for example, of informed consent, have been linked to potential participants having little experience of research methods and poor literacy as well as the impenetrability of the language of Western ethics. Tensions have also been linked to the ethical standards needed for publication in the "Global North". This leaves ethnographers, wishing to represent and give voice to cultures in such contexts, with ethical work to do in ensuring they feel their ethical practice is culturally appropriate. The chapter by Fox and Mitchell (Chapter 8) examines such work in the context of a study undertaken in a school in Tigray, Ethiopia.

According to Kitchener and Kitchener (2009), ethical principles can be theorised in a fourth level of decision-making and, above this, be problematised and defined in a fifth layer of meta-ethical decision-making. Chapters in this book related to theorisations as they apply to ethnography include Beach and Arrazola's exploration of how post-humanist and critical ontologies extend and challenge existing theoretical stances and Fox and Mitchell's exploration of a multi-theoretical model to support ethical reflexivity. Traianou's chapter takes a fourth-level analysis by focusing on presenting and unpicking a key meta-ethical concept relevant to ethnography: that of *phrónēsis*.

The relationship between principles and ethical theories is not straightforward. In an increasingly globalised and diverse world of social science researchers, there is an associated increased lack of theoretical agreement amongst researchers and an increasingly diverse range of contexts in which to consider what constitutes culturally appropriate research behaviour. A selected review of recent academics' work shows the range of theoretical traditions that are perceived as relevant to social science research. Table 1.2 summarises the range of theoretical and philosophical stances used by some academics to explain the generation of principles relevant to research with human participants.

Table 1.2 Analysis of key ethical theories covered by selected academics

Key ethical theories/authors	Israel (2015)	Kitchener and Kitchener (2009)	Brooks, de Riele and Maguire (2014)	Mustajoki and Mustajoki (2017)	Farrimond (2012)	Hammersley and Traianou (2012, 2014)
Consequentialism/ utilitarianism	*	*	*	*	*	*
Non-consequentialism	*					
Principalism	*			*		
Virtue	*	*	*	*	*	*
Casuistry	*					
Critical (also feminism, ethic of care, and situated)	*	*				*
Contractarianism		*				
Deontology		*	*		*	*
Justice						*

These principles come from very different traditions and rationales for how researchers "ought" to behave to be considered ethical. Flinders (1992) drew together four such theoretical stances to compare the implications of each for principled practices at different stages of a research project (Table 1.3). This framework is explored and critiqued further in the chapter in this book by Beach and Arrazola (Chapter 3). It can be noted that whilst three of the traditions Flinders pulled together are also represented in Table 1.2, an additional ecological perspective is included that takes account of the need for researchers to be aware of and respond to local, contextual factors and norms. For qualitative enquiry relevant to educational research Flinders pointed to how the relational and ecological stances offer more appropriate ethical bases for studies as compared with utilitarian and deontological approaches. He argues the latter have been shown to have failed to be inclusive in protecting the rights of those already marginalised by society, whereas social scientific enquiry should work towards meeting the needs and interests of all. Similarly, critical and feminist-based enquiries seek to go beyond avoiding inequality such that their studies contribute to addressing such injustices (Beach & Eriksson 2010). After comparing Flinders' advice on alternative stances with a framework offered by Seedhouse (1998), Fox and Stutchbury (2009) concluded that rather than being incompatible with one another, these four traditions offered alternative lenses which, together, can support comprehensive ethical appraisal of a study. Their deliberative, rather than prescriptive, framework is applied in Fox and Mitchell's chapter (Chapter 8) to support ethical reflexivity throughout an ethnographic study in an Ethiopian school (see Table 1.3).

In terms of the application of theoretical traditions of thinking to ethnographic studies, different ethnographic traditions also draw on different traditions, depending on whether, for example, interactionist, critical, feminist or micro-ethnographic approaches are adopted (Beach & Eriksson 2010). There has been a call by some for there to be an ethical turn such that ethnography searches for a common basis and for this to be more confidently reflexive and consultative

Table 1.3 Table of ethical guidelines for fieldwork

Theoretical tradition/stages of a research project	Utilitarian	Deontological	Relational	Ecological
Recruitment	Informed consent	Reciprocity	Collaboration	Cultural sensitivity
Fieldwork	Avoidance of harm	Avoidance of wrong	Avoidance of imposition	Avoidance of detachment
Reporting	Confidentiality	Fairness	Confirmation	Responsive communication

Source: Flinders (1992: 113).

theoretically. This accepts and recognises the variety of potentially competing values and norms to be found not only in the web of obligations discussed as part of level-two ethical deliberation but also to properly prioritise the diversity of needs, interests and views of those in the research setting itself (Beach & Eriksson 2010; Gewirtz & Cribb 2008; Gudmundsdottir 1990). Recent thinking about a "new ethics" argues that researchers and the researched should be put on a more equal footing and principles (or even theories) of justice and care should be used to transform the very goals of research as well as how ethnographic studies are carried out (Hammersley & Traianou 2014). It is argued that, to ensure some of those in the setting to be studied are not silenced and are given voice, there should be a "response-ability" in the research (Beach & Eriksson 2010: 132). This would require in-vivo, reflective and negotiated ways of working to develop in a way which would not be possible if only predetermined ethical practices are relied upon as models of research behaviours. This leads us on to the practical wisdom generated as phronesis in ethnographic fieldwork discussed by Traianou in this book, which needs to be developed and articulated by ethnographers and trusted by regulatory boards. The self-reflexivity required by researchers can be considered part of the relational work of ethnographic enquiry, if intra-personal as well as inter-personal enquiry is pursued and values and assumptions properly problematised (Dennis 2018). Such self-reflexivity will arguably allow ethnographers to acknowledge the biases they bring, which might even be termed "lies" they might otherwise unconsciously embody (Fine 1993).

This book contributes chapters advocating the wide scope for such ethical reflexivity in relation to embarking on ethnography and its implications for regulation and practice – a reflexivity strongly defended as necessary for all social science research (Gewirtz & Cribb 2006, 2008). This allows illustration of different methodological applications of ethnography, including engaging with current debates on what counts as ethical applications of different forms of ethnography such as how political ethnography can be through whether researchers intend transformation or a somewhat more independent representation (Beach & Eriksson 2010; Hammersley 2006).

Concerning the chapters

The chapters of this book arise out of a symposium on the practice of ethics in educational ethnographic research held at the European Conference on Educational Research (ECER) in Copenhagen, 2017. The conference is run by the European Educational Research Association (EERA). The symposium emerged from online discussions by members of Network 19 of the Conference Ethnography in Education, chaired by Sofia Marques da Silva in 2017, in the months before the conference, as did the coordination of the symposium by the editors of this book. Contributors to the symposium, as also to this book, came from many European countries, including Norway, Finland, Sweden, Spain and the UK, as well as the USA.

Table 1.4 The six questions guiding authors in this book

1 What can we (ethnographers, members of academia, members of the public) expect and not expect of ethical review boards?
2 Where are the spaces for and with whom should dialogue take place about ethicality in our research?
3 What effect does a research topic's focus have on both dealing with regulation and research practice?
4 What effect does context have on researchers' ethical practices?
5 What effect does the positionality of a researcher have on ethical practices?
6 How do we ensure that ethicality supports the trustworthiness of research projects?

Through the course of the conversations during the conference, six questions emerged inductively – see Table 1.4 – about the application of ethical practice in educational ethnography. These have been used to varying degrees by authors of the chapters in this book to guide the development of their contributions.

Although most of the chapters address only two or three of these questions, they generally all refer to the regulatory ethical procedures which envelop the practices of researchers, especially those in their own countries. This helps to make visible the variety of regulatory practices pursued in different European countries.

Part I of the book, on "Informing compliance with regulation", see question one above, has two chapters which focus critically on regulatory ethical procedures and what researchers and the general public might expect from them. In the chapters by Beach and Arrazola (Chapter 3) and by Traianou (Chapter 2) the relevance of these regulatory practices to ethnographic research are challenged, arguing that the over-formalisation of processes for gaining informed consent from participants and for recording, that researchers know how to do this effectively, risks inhibiting the development of research projects that do not use a medical/scientific approach to research. On the other hand, they acknowledge that research project participants and the public, as well as other beneficiaries of research, need to be reassured that any research project is carried out ethically to protect effectively from harm its participants and their environments, and to produce trustworthy findings.

However, concern with formalised regulatory procedures runs throughout the book. In Chapter 4 in Part II of the book, "Applying ethics in the field", Smette enhances this scepticism about formalised regulatory practices and procedures pointing out that they do not really work well with those types of research, such as educational ethnography, which require researchers to re-negotiate informed consent with their participants as the process of a study unfolds and, possibly, the participants in a study alter – a view with which Nikkanen and Dovemark concur in their chapters (Chapters 6 and 7, respectively) in Part III on "Ethical dilemmas in the field".

Several chapters discuss in what spaces and with which people should dialogues about the ethics of research be carried out. Fox and Mitchell, in Chapter 8 in Part III, argue that these spaces can be constructed with other research workers to help researchers think reflexively about their work and the application of ethics within it. However, they point out that the scope of the reflections needs to be bounded if it is not to become overwhelming and a hinderance to practice. They argue that reflexivity should help a researcher to focus on the enactment of ethical practices in a project and how to give account of those to research authorities such as ethical review boards who license practitioners to carry out projects. In other chapters, Smette and Nikkanen also argue that reflexive spaces allow researchers to work out practical solutions to their ethical dilemmas, pointing out that ethical review bodies in their countries include in their regulatory function acting as a sounding board for researchers to develop their practices for their studies, an approach which Traianou also commends in her arguments (Chapter 2). Other chapters by Busher (Chapter 5), and by Beach and Arrazola (Chapter 3) argue that reflexive spaces for researchers need to be constructed with research project participants and gatekeepers who control access to a research site and/or to participants in it. These, the authors argue, are the people with whom researchers need to have discussions about how to construct ethical research practice for a project on a particular site.

Turning to the chapters in specific sections of the book: in Part I, "Informing compliance with regulation", there are two chapters, one by Traianou (Chapter 2) and one by Beach and Arrazola (Chapter 3). Traianou discusses ways of lessening the tension between the approaches to ethical regulation that has crept into the social sciences from medicine and psychology and the practical requirements of carrying out educational ethnography in an ethical manner. She argues that the dominant discourses for thinking about ethical regulation are highly problematic as they assume that what is needed is the application of general principles to specific situations that can be transformed into procedural certainties that institutional regulatory bodies for ethics can monitor. However, this approach is fundamentally at odds, she argues, with ethnographic research where each project is a unique experience that challenges a researcher's understanding and judgement of ethical practice in the field. This understanding of research has resonances with the idea of phronesis, she argues. Phronesis offers a process of interpretation of situations that requires skilful practice by researchers to make virtuous judgements in the field, rather than relying on proceduralist structures managed by committees to construct ethical ethnographic research. Research ethics committees could play a part in this by encouraging researchers to develop these skills, as they appear to do in Finland and Sweden.

Beach and Arrazola discuss critically the role that ethical regulation through institutional review boards plays with researchers seeking legitimation for their research projects. They point out that being ethical as an educational ethnographer is not isolated from how people engage as ethical beings with others in the world but may be related to the research methodologies researchers choose to use. This, they argue, has led many educational ethnographers to question the value of ethical review boards, coming to see the process of ethical approval as merely a bureaucratic hoop to be jumped through. However, Beach and Arrazola (Chapter 3), using examples from Spain and Sweden, consider ethical review boards as necessary but needing to take more account of the situatedness, post-qualitative and post-humanist dimensions of ethics when deciding whether or not to approve the ethical practices of a proposed research project. According to these authors, ethical practices are forged in the interpersonal interactions of everyday life influenced by participants' commitments to a variety of scientific, ideological and political goals, beliefs and practices.

In Part II, "Applying ethics in the field", there are two chapters, one by Smette (Chapter 4) and one by Busher (Chapter 5). Smette argues that require-ments by research ethics committees for researchers to obtain consent from all potential participants before the start of a study make it impossible to do eth-nographic research in institutional settings. Drawing on her experiences from researching in secondary schools in Norway, she discusses the ethical dilemmas and the methodological and analytical challenges posed by participant obser-vation when not all pupils and parents choose to take part in a study. The dilemmas arise, she argues, because social practices in public institutions, such as schools, need to be discussed publicly and the interests of individuals not to take part cannot override the public interest in knowing what is taking place on those sites. Formalised approaches to gaining prior informed consent from participants do not address the dilemmas ethnographic researchers face, espe-cially, as she points out, as people's decisions not to take part in a project can be time-related and may change, and therefore can be renegotiated as a research project progresses. Consequently, ethnographers need to continue to reflect on how to observe and ethically represent collectives that include individuals who do not wish to participate.

Busher focuses on how to protect and involve vulnerable participants in research, noting that vulnerability is not just a consequence of personal attributes but of the ways in which researchers choose to carry out projects. What factors contribute to participants being deemed vulnerable in a research project are developed by considering how the processes of consent are nego-tiated with participants and how different research methodologies can make participants vulnerable by making them more or less visible. Arguing that researchers have a responsibility for protecting research participants from harm throughout the life of a project and afterwards when it is written up, Busher discusses how researchers might move beyond a protective duty of care to help vulnerable participants engage healthfully with research projects so that their involvement helps them to develop their identities and agency as people. This approach to practice in the field goes beyond what is often required by institutional ethical codes of keeping participants safe from harm and requires researchers to consider reflexively throughout the life of a research project how to implement ethical practice in the field.

In Part III, "Ethical dilemmas in the field", there are three chapters: one by Nikkanen (Chapter 6), one by Dovemark (Chapter 7), and one by Fox and Mitchell (Chapter 8). Nikkanen focuses on the ethical dilemmas encountered by a teacher-researcher carrying out ethnographic research in Finnish secondary comprehensive schools. Her dual role allows her to live in "the field" for years, gaining tacit knowledge of the profession, and following the societal and educational changes in the school in real time. However, she points out that her double position raises ethical questions about how to record the daily life of a school as an observing researcher while sustaining her teaching commitments as an equal and active member of school staff and confronting the ethical dilemmas of students' consent/non-consent to participation in her research. However, she notes that in Finland teacher ethics are even stricter than researcher ethics when it comes to protecting teachers and students from harm. She concludes by hoping that teacher researchers can act as active agents for participatory practices and positive change in both fields, but acknowledges that they risk being perceived as spies if colleagues or students feel that anything they say may be used for unknown purposes. This dual role, she suggests, needs a special sensitivity for choosing appropriate research topics and methods.

Dovemark focuses on the ethical dilemmas raised by carrying out ethnography in semi-public contexts that are nationally relevant but insufficiently studied in relation to the marketised Swedish educational system. Citing venues like upper-secondary school fairs and open houses where schools can market themselves and lure customers, she notes that researchers can access these "semi"-public events, without gaining direct consent from participants, and write field notes based on their experiences and overheard conversations on how people choosing schools act and how different schools market themselves. The problems she notes are whether such research practices are ethical, occurring as they do in a semi-public arena where it is not always possible for a researcher to be able to obtain informed consent in advance, and how researchers find a reasonable balance between the interests of different people, including the quest for new knowledge from under-researched but socially important sites like the one she exemplifies.

Fox and Mitchell focus on ethical learning through developing an educational ethnography. They use the vehicle of doctoral research supervision to show how ethical learning is related to ethnographic methodology, project planning, fieldwork and reporting in an international context. After discussing the CERD ethical framework as a tool to scaffold learning about ethical practice, they show how support was given to a doctoral researcher through a series of meetings focused on ethical issues. These meetings allowed Mitchell to rehearse and become confident in his ethical stance and behaviours. The authors also note, however, that the supervisor, too, learnt from the experience about ethnography and cultural sensitivity in a particular setting with which she was practically unfamiliar. In their chapter, they offer an account of the use of extended dialogue focused on ethical reflexivity to create explicit, meaningful and mutual understanding of issues relating to a research project, in this case an ethnographic study of schools in Ethiopia. The authors argue that the process helped to deepen their understanding of ethical practices in educational ethnography and the effective use of the ethical framework itself for their own further work.

The last chapter, in a section on its own, offers a critical synthesis of the preceding chapters. Dennis draws together the themes that have emerged in the book and shows how they are reflected in different chapters. In doing so, Dennis explains how she thinks ethical discussions about ethical practices in educational ethnography are developing.

References

Academy of Social Sciences (AcSS). 2015. *Five Ethical Principles for Social Science Research.* London: AcSS. Available at: www.acss.org.uk/wp-content/uploads/2016/06/5-Ethics-Principles-for-Social-Science-Research-Flyer.pdf.

All European Academies (ALLEA). 2017. *The European Code of Conduct for Research Integrity.* Berlin: European Science Foundation. Available at: https://ec.europa.eu/research/participants/data/ref/h2020/other/hi/h2020-ethics_code-of-conduct_en.pdf.

American Educational Research Association (AERA). 2011. "Code of Ethics". *Educational Researcher* 40(3): 145–156.

Beach, D. and Eriksson, A. 2010. "The relationship between ethical positions and methodological approaches: A Scandinavian perspective". *Ethnography and Education* 5(2): 129–142.

British Educational Research Association (BERA). 2018. *Ethical Guidelines for Educational Research.* 4th edn. London: BERA. Available at: www.bera.ac.uk/wp-content/uploads/2018/06/BERA-Ethical-Guidelines-for-Educational-Research_4thEdn_2018.pdf?noredirect=1.

Brooks, R., de Riele, K. and Maguire, M. 2014. *Ethics and Educational Research.* London: British Educational Research Association.

Canadian Institutes of Health Research (CIHR), Natural Sciences and Engineering Research Council (NSERC) and Social Sciences and Humanities Research Council (SSHRC). 2010. *Tri-Council Policy Statement: Ethical Conduct for Research Involving Humans (TCPS2).* Available at: http://ethics.gc.ca/eng/policy-politique/initiatives/tcps2-eptcs2/default/.

Chilisa, B. 2009. "Indigenous African-centred ethics: Contesting and complementing dominant models". In *Handbook of Social Research Ethics,* edited by D.M. Mertens and P.E. Ginsberg, 407–425. Thousand Oaks, CA: Sage.

Conselho Nacional de Saude (CNdeS). 2012. *Resolution 466 Diretrizes e Normas Regulamentado-ras de Pesquisas Envolvendo Seres Humanos.* Brazil: CNS. Available at: http://conselho.saude.gov.br/resolucoes/2012/Reso466.pdf.

Department of Health, Education and Welfare (DHEW). 1979. *The Belmont Report: Ethical Principles and Guidelines of the Protection of Human Subjects of Research.* Washington, DC: DHEW. Available at: www.hhs.gov/ohrp/humansubjects/guidance/belmont.html.

Dennis, B. 2018. "Tales of working without/against a compass: Rethinking ethical dilemmas in educational ethnography". In *The Wiley Handbook of Ethnography of Education*, edited by D. Beach, C. Bagley and S. Marques da Silva, 51–70. New York and London: Wiley.

Economic and Social Research Council (ESRC). 2018. *Our Core Principles*. London: ESRC. Available at: https://esrc.ukri.org/funding/guidance-for-applicants/research-ethics/our-core-principles/.

Farrimond, H. 2012. *Doing Ethical Research*. London: Palgrave.

Fine, G.A. 1993. "Ten lies of ethnography". *Journal of Contemporary Ethnography* 22: 267–294.

Flinders, D. 1992. "In search of ethical guidance: Constructing a basis for dialogue". *Qualitative Studies in Education* 5(2): 101–115.

Gewirtz, S. and Cribb, A. 2006. "What to do about values in social research: The case for ethical reflexivity in the sociology of education". *British Journal of Sociology of Education* 27(2): 141–155.

Gewirtz, S. and Cribb, A. 2008. "Differing to agree: A reply to Hammersley and Abraham". *British Journal of Sociology of Education* 29(5): 559–562.

Gudmundsdottir, S. 1990. "Values in pedagogical content knowledge". *Journal of Teacher Education* 41(3): 44–52.

Hammersley, M. 2006. "Ethnography: Problems and prospects". *Ethnography and Education* 1(1): 3–14.

Hammersley, M. and Traianou, A. 2012. *Ethics in Qualitative Research: Controversies and Contexts*. London: Sage.

Hammersley, M. and Traianou, A. 2014. "An alternative ethics? Justice and care as guiding principles for qualitative research". *Sociological Research Online* 19(3): 24.

Israel, M. 2015. *Research Ethics and Integrity for Social Scientists*. 2nd edn. London: Sage.

Kitchener, K.S. and Kitchener, R.F. 2009. "Social science research ethics: Historical and philosophical issues". In *The Handbook of Social Research Ethics*, edited by D.M. Mertens and P.E. Ginsberg, 5–22. New York: Sage.

Mustajoki, H. and Mustajoki, A. 2017. *A New Approach to Research Ethics: Using Guided Dialogue to Strengthen Research Communities*. London: Routledge.

National Health and Medical Research Council (NHMRC), Australian Research Council (ARC) and Australian Vice Chancellors' Committee (AVCC). 2007 (updated 2018). *National Statement on Ethical Conduct in Human Research*. Canberra: NHMRC, ARC and AVCC. Available at: www.nhmrc.gov.au/guidelines-publications/e72.

Nuremberg Code (agreed 1947; published 1949) "Permissible medical experiments". In Trials of War Criminals before the Nuremberg Military Tribunals under Control Council Law 10(2): 181–182. Washington, DC: US Government Printing Office.

Qureshi, R. 2011. "Who pays the price? The ethics of vulnerability in research". In *Research Methodologies in the 'South'*, edited by A. Halai and D. Wiliam, 90–116. Oxford: Oxford University Press.

Rashid, M., Cain, V. and Goez, H. 2015. "The encounters and challenges of ethnography as a methodology in health research". *International Journal of Qualitative Methods* 1(1): 1–16.

Seedhouse, D. 1998. *Ethics: The Heart of Healthcare*. Chichester: Wiley.

Stutchbury, K. and Fox, A. 2009. "Ethics in educational research: Introducing a methodological tool for effective ethical analysis". *Cambridge Journal of Education* 39(4): 489–504.

Wiliam, D. 2011. "Logic, observation, representation, dialectic and ethical values: What counts as evidence in educational research?" In *Research Methodologies in the 'South'*, edited by A. Halai and D. Wiliam, 245–257. Oxford: Oxford University Press.

World Conference on Research Integrity. 2010. *The Singapore Statement*. Available at: https://wcrif.org/guidance/singapore-statement.

World Medical Association (WMA). 2013. *Declaration of Helsinki: Medical Research Involving Human Subjects*. Available at: www.wma.net/what-we-do/medical-ethics/declaration-of-helsinki/.

Part I

Informing compliance with regulation

Chapter 2

Phrónēsis and the ethical regulation of ethnographic research

Anna Traianou

Introduction

In Western societies, ethical regulation spread out from medicine and research in psychology to other areas, so that it now covers virtually all of social science. This occurred some time ago in the USA, with the operational field of institutional review boards (IRBs), which were set up in the wake of the Belmont Report in 1979, gradually being extended. What has been referred to as "ethics creep" is a more recent development in the UK, and some other countries, such as Canada, Australia and New Zealand, and at European Union level in the context of applying for research funding, but the process is much the same (see Haggerty 2004; van den Hoonaard & Hamilton 2016). Ethical regulation involves IRBs or research ethics committees (RECs) in universities and other institutions exercising mandatory, pre-emptive control over research by academic researchers. They must submit outlines of their proposed investigations that identify any potential ethical problems likely to arise, and how they plan to deal with them. In response, IRBs/RECs decide whether all the problems have been recognised, whether the proposed solutions are acceptable, and therefore whether the research can proceed.

Ethical regulation of this kind had its origins in genuine concerns about serious ethical failings in the pursuit of medical research (Dingwall 2012). However, there has been little attempt to demonstrate that social research suffers from ethical problems that are so serious as to require this draconian form of control. Furthermore, it has been argued that, far from increasing the methodological and ethical quality of social research, ethical regulation is either ineffective or actually damaging (see, for example, Shweder 2006; Hamburger 2007; Hammersley 2009; Katz 2007; Schrag 2010; van den Hoonaard 2011; van den Hoonaard & Hamilton 2016; Traianou 2018). Further, it has been recognised that ethical regulation causes particular problems for ethnographic research (see Delamont & Atkinson 2018), for example, the tendency of IRBs/RECs to require that written informed consent is secured before research begins. These requirements make it difficult for ethnographers to obtain authorisation without distorting their work. While it may be accepted that achieving fully informed and free consent is an ideal that is not always possible to achieve, and perhaps even that covert inquiry may under some (rare) circumstances be legitimate, ethnography is generally framed by ethical regulation regimes as non-standard and marginal.

The emphasis given to obtaining informed consent by IRBs/RECs arises, to a large extent, from a proceduralist approach to ethics on their part. This involves treating ethical conduct as if it were a matter of complying with standard rules or procedures. This approach has become prevalent across business and the professions, for instance, in the form of "ethical audit" (see Baggini 2018). It fits closely with wider efforts to make the work of occupational practitioners "transparently accountable", in both public and private organisations. Pressure for this derives from the fact that the second half of the twentieth century witnessed a gradual erosion of public trust in claims made by professionals to be devoted solely to carrying out their tasks well, and thereby in their capacity to regulate themselves (see Pollitt 1990; Whitty 2000). Indeed, some economists and sociologists came to view professionalism as an ideology designed to enable occupations to increase their power over clients, over other occupations, and in relation to other organisations, including nation-states (see, for example, Larson 1977). At the same time, this emphasis on "transparent accountability" reflects the fact that – in the context of large, complex, and to a large degree globalised, societies – we are forced to rely upon anonymous others, where there can be no personal trust. While professional status and expertise at one time provided a substitute for this, this kind of trust is undercut in a world where status hierarchies are increasingly under challenge, and where trust has been eroded by fraudulent advertising and political spin. The rise of ethical regulation reflects this development, along with the associated concern of funders and universities with the threat of litigation.

While IRBs/RECs may show some flexibility in dealing with particular projects, then, their fundamental mode of operation is proceduralist, and this is virtually unavoidable given the task assigned to them (van den Hoonaard 2011; Stark 2011). Moreover, from a proceduralist point of view, ethnography does not, and probably cannot, meet the ethical requirements that ought to guide social research. In particular, it involves initial planning but not a detailed plan that is ethically sound which is then executed. Instead, the research process evolves, adapting to changes not only in the situations being investigated but also in conceptualisation of the problems that are the focus of inquiry. In these terms, ethnography can easily be seen as intrinsically unethical.

Yet, serious questions can be raised about this proceduralist approach to ethics. Even philosophical discussions of ethics that focus on the role of general principles generally recognise that applying these to particular situations will involve considerable interpretation, and indeed flexibility (see Hammersley & Traianou 2012: chapter 1). Furthermore, there are ethics writers who challenge the relevance even of general principles, arguing that ethical judgement is necessarily situationally variable or context-dependent (Dancy 2004). In this chapter, I draw on an approach of this kind, virtue ethics, and in particular on the Aristotelian concept of *phrónēsis*, which has become increasingly influential in the literature on research ethics today (Macfarlane 2009; Emmerich 2018). This is an approach that is much more compatible with ethnography than is proceduralism.

What is *phrónēsis*?

Aristotle argued that all forms of governance – from state decision-making to the running of a household – rely on *phrónēsis*. One translation of this Greek word would be "skill", especially since today we talk of social as well as of physical skills. It is significant that skills are acquired via lengthy periods of practice, perhaps via some kind of apprenticeship or simply through first-hand experience, along with reflection on this directed towards facilitating improved performance. The concept of skill captures an important aspect of the meaning of *phrónēsis*: that successful practice does not amount to following a set of rules, even though "rules of thumb" can be used to facilitate and refine this (see Dreyfus & Dreyfus 1986; Dreyfus 2004; see also Eraut 1994). Rather, skilful practice involves situationally appropriate decision-making that takes account of all relevant, and only of relevant, considerations.

However, the notion of skill omits something important from the meaning given to the term *phrónēsis* by Aristotle; for him, it refers to a pre-eminent virtue (see Hammersley 2018; Pring 2001; Macfarlane 2009; MacIntyre 1981). What Aristotle means by an activity being done well is not just that actions are effective in achieving a goal but that they are performed in ways that are good in a broader sense: that they exemplify and respect the human ideal. An important part of this is that how activity is performed must be good for the person engaged in it; it must form part of a good life for that person. Aristotle argues that only those who act in ways that contribute to a good life for themselves will be acting ethically. Indeed, this is in large part what the term "ethical" means for him.

The notion of *phrónēsis* has been selectively interpreted and widely applied in seeking to understand the character of professional work of various kinds, from educational and business leadership to medical training, urban planning or policymaking (Krajewski 2011). Furthermore, it has often been mobilised to resist attempts to impose technical or ethical regulations of various sorts on professionals. It has been argued that such regulations are incompatible with the very nature of professional work, and that attempts to impose them will necessarily distort it (see Dunne 1997). In these terms, we can think of human activities as ranged along a dimension of increasing complexity, so that the more complex the activity, the greater the need for the exercise of *phrónēsis*. What "complexity" refers to here is the degree of uncertainty surrounding the nature of the situation faced, and the implications of relevant principles for that situation. The effect of a high degree of complexity is that considerable interpretation and judgement are required in order to accomplish the activity effectively. Good decision-making must draw on past experience of similar situations and take into account all relevant concerns, and conflicts amongst them. While it may be possible to reduce pursuit of some activities to specific procedures or rules (e.g., reciting a poem or carrying out a statistical test), this is not possible in the case of many others. The latter are not susceptible to a proceduralist approach, and attempts to organise and control them in this fashion are likely to be counterproductive. There are clear parallels here with the criticisms made of ethical regulation by ethnographers.

The conflict between *phrónēsis* and ethical regulation of research

Pre-emptive ethical regulation is at odds with the idea that researchers must exercise *phrónēsis* since to a large extent it demands compliance with pre-specified rules. In this respect, as I indicated, there is an inevitable tendency for such regulation to operate on the basis of a proceduralist conception of ethics. This tendency arises from the fact that few members of IRBs/RECs will have direct experience of all the kinds of research method to be used in the proposals about which they must make decisions. And, equally important in the case of ethnography, they will often have little familiarity with the sorts of situation in which the research is to be carried out. This encourages recourse to general rules, a tendency that is reinforced by the commitment to a "transparent" mode of operation. The rules concerned, for example, as enshrined in various research ethics "codes", amount to an "abridgement of the contingencies and vicissitudes of practice that aspires to be, but can never succeed in becoming, an authoritative, prescriptive guide for practice" (Gray 2009: 78–79).[1]

Perhaps the most fundamental problem is that regulatory regimes are pre-emptive or anticipatory; they assume that ethical issues can be identified at the beginning of the research process and properly addressed there and then. Hence, ethics committees will only approve a project if potential ethical and indeed methodological problems, along with strategies for dealing with them, have been explicitly identified at the start. Researchers have become all too familiar with the "ethical clearance" forms that they have to submit. Yet it is obvious, even from the most superficial experience of the research process, that not all problems can be anticipated, that some which are anticipated do not arise and that even when problems have been anticipated they will often take forms that require new thinking about how to handle them in the specific circumstances in which they occur.

And, of course, this is especially true in the case of ethnographic inquiry. It cannot involve formulating a research design at the beginning, and then simply implementing it. Participant observation in natural settings requires continual negotiation of access to data, and is therefore subject to various contingencies, over many of which the researcher has little control. Access often depends on the ethnographers' capacity for sustaining the cooperation of the participants; and the latter can be, and sometimes is, withdrawn (see, for example, Traianou 2007). Consent tends to be negotiated and renegotiated over time as the relationship between the ethnographer and the research participants develops (Murphy & Dingwall 2007). Even in the case of interviews, these are usually relatively unstructured in character, so that what particular questions will be asked and what will be said cannot be anticipated; and, often, they are carried out in settings that are not controlled by the researcher, such as school staffrooms, classrooms, or playgrounds. All these features make it difficult to anticipate what will happen at various stages of the research process and to plan in any detail for how ethical issues will be dealt with.

Also at odds with the idea that researchers must exercise *phrónēsis* is the assumption, frequently built into ethical regulation, that "best practice" in research can be pre-specified. This is not possible because, like many other professional activities, research is a form of *praxis*. The grounds for decisions cannot be made fully explicit in ways that would be accessible to someone with little experience of the kind of research involved and/or of the situation in which it was carried out. There is a parallel here with the difficulty teachers sometimes experience in explaining the decisions they make in the classroom (see Traianou 2006) or that doctors face explaining in "transparent" terms how they judge what particular sets of symptoms indicate, and why. This does not suggest that these matters are beyond all expression, only that tacit knowledge and understanding are involved (see Montgomery 2006).

We should also note that there is a tendency for IRBs/RECs, given their particular responsibilities, to give more weight to ethical than to other relevant considerations. This can often result in what has been called moralism: "the vice of overdoing morality" (Coady 2005: 101; Hammersley & Traianou 2012: conclusion).[2] One manifestation of this is the common requirement that researchers adhere to "high", perhaps even to "the highest", ethical standards, these being specified in terms of abstract principles whose implications for particular cases are regarded as closely determined – in effect, they amount to injunctions. Appeal to high, or even to the highest, ethical standards is routine in the rhetoric around ethical regulation. For example, the UK Research Integrity Office states that "we promote integrity and high ethical standards", and it recently produced a document which places emphasis on the "training and development" of researchers in order to ensure that they meet the "highest standards" of "research conduct".[3] This document is entirely about compliance, with no hint that there could be problems or disagreements about what would and would not be ethical, or what would be justifiable in broader terms, as regards social research. For instance, one concrete requirement is that fully informed consent be obtained from all research participants (p. 14). In a similar way, for all research projects funded by the European Union under Horizon 2020: "ethics is an integral part of research from beginning to end, and ethical compliance is seen as pivotal to achieve real research excellence".[4]

Yet, as has been argued elsewhere, seeking written consent from participants is not always desirable (see Hammersley & Traianou 2012: chapter 4). Indeed, it is far from clear that informed consent of any kind is *always* required. Thus, a case can even be made for covert research in some circumstances. While some commentators have argued that it is virtually never legitimate (Bok 1978; Shils 1956; Warwick 1982; Homan 1980), others have challenged this (Calvey 2000,

2008, 2017; Roulet et al. 2017). These discussions have identified a range of considerations that need to be taken into account in making judgements about this issue. What this indicates is that, rather than being formulated either as a general prohibition, or even as a globally permissive statement, any judgement about whether or not covert research is legitimate must be made in relation to specific cases (see Bulmer et al. 1982). This is because covertness can vary significantly in degree and character, as also can conditions in the field that are relevant to making a judgement about its legitimacy, such as the vulnerability or power of the people being studied.

In statements like those from the UKRIO and Horizon 2020, mentioned earlier, it is apparently assumed that we cannot be "too ethical", and that social research involves a high risk of severe ethical dangers for the people studied, so that rigorous precautions must be taken to avoid these. Yet, the presence of these severe dangers has not been demonstrated, and, since there are often conflicting principles, it is by no means clear what would or would not be ethical, or more rather than less ethical, in some cases. Furthermore, there is very often a tension between ethical considerations relating to the people being studied and the methodological requirements of the research, so that some sort of trade-off is required between the two. Once again, this must necessarily be done in a way that takes account of the distinctive features of the particular situation(s) faced. For reasons already explained, this is not the sort of judgement that ethics committees can make, nor that can be framed in terms of rules.

It is also necessary to recognise that in the world in which researchers must operate the other parties with whom they have to deal may well be committed to ideals and interests, or engage in behaviour, that are at odds with the requirements of social research, to one degree or another. One of the problems with the kind of moralism underpinning ethical regulation being criticised here is that it is premised on an unrealistic view of human nature and society. Conflicting ideals and interests, and struggles over these, are endemic in social life; and, as a result, the use of coercion, manipulation, and deception is widespread. Given this, moralism is not a viable basis for carrying out any activity, including ethnographic inquiry (Douglas 1976; Duster, Matza & Wellman 1979; Littrell 1993). If researchers are to get their work done in the world as it is, and produce reliable knowledge, they will often have to engage in actions that fall short of the highest standards specified in moral codes or guidance provided by regulatory regimes.

In short, what can reasonably be expected of ethnographers is *not* compliance with the highest ethical standards but rather that their behaviour is *acceptable* in terms of the whole range of practical values involved, taking account of the constraints operating in the situations concerned. It is also important to remember that social scientists are members of a profession operating *within* societies and that all they can distinctively aspire to is a high commitment to a specific goal and to the values associated with this, not some general ethical superiority. Perhaps it is necessary to emphasise that this does not amount to a recommendation of expediency, even less to the conclusion that "anything goes".

In fact, adopting a more realistic conception of what research ethics entails ought to lead to more careful and realistic judgements about what can and should be done in the field.

Interestingly, all this suggests a slightly different approach to the notion of *phrónēsis* from that characteristic of Aristotle, one that takes in Machiavelli's rather different conception of "virtue". Contrary to what is sometimes assumed, Machiavelli did not propose that rulers and other political agents should pursue evil ends. Rather, he argued that they will often have to use means that are regarded as morally questionable, such as deception, and even sometimes those that are abhorrent, like war, in order effectively to pursue ends that are good. According to Strauss (1987: 84), Machiavelli was the first of the early modern political philosophers, whose ethical thinking starts not from "how people ought to live", in the manner of the ancients, but rather from "how people actually live". In Max Weber's terms, Machiavelli rejected an "ethics of ultimate ends" in favour of an "ethics of responsibility" (see Bruun 2007: 250–259). It seems to me that there is scope for applying this argument in the context of research (Hammersley & Traianou 2011).

However, the contrast between this Machiavellian approach and the Aristotelian notion of *phrónēsis* should not be exaggerated; in both cases the emphasis is on the need to develop wise and skilful judgement in dealing, in the best way possible, with the contingencies that arise, taking account of all the considerations that are relevant, including those that conflict with one another. This is not a matter of the end justifying the use of any means, but rather that both ends and means must be ranked in terms of desirability (on various grounds), with *phrónēsis* being deployed to "weigh" the relative desirability of achieving a particular end against the use of means of varying degrees of likely effectiveness and desirability.

Conclusion

I have argued that the spread of ethical regulation to social research has been closely associated with the broader demand for transparent accountability within governments and other large organisations, in both the public and private sectors. This demand is understandable. The second half of the twentieth century witnessed a gradual erosion of public trust in claims made by professionals to be devoted solely to carrying out their tasks well, and thereby in their capacity to regulate themselves. Indeed, some sociologists and economists came to view professionalism as an ideology designed to enable occupations to increase their power over clients, over other occupations, and in relation to other organisations, including nation-states (see, for example, Larson 1977). In this context, it might be argued that use of the concept of *phrónēsis* amounts to little more than an appeal to professional mystique, allowing bias in the service of self-interest.

In the context of large, complex and to a large degree globalised societies, we are forced to rely on anonymous others, where there can be no personal trust (Power 1997). While professional status and expertise at one time provided a substitute for this, in a world where status hierarchies are increasingly under challenge, and where trust has been eroded by fraudulent advertising and political spin, this kind of trust is undercut. As a result, there have been increasing demands for "transparent accountability", in other words that the basis for professional judgements be made explicit so as to be open to judgement by lay people. This was, of course, a central theme in the evidence-based practice movement (Wieringa et al. 2017). While such accountability may not be possible, as I have argued here, the concerns lying behind the call for it are genuine.

Furthermore, there are certainly potentially serious ethical dangers involved in the pursuit of some kinds of research; and, where these arise, regulation will certainly be necessary. But it has not been established that social research involves dangers of such severity that mandatory, pre-emptive ethical regulation is required. Nor has such regulation been shown to be effective in reducing these dangers. As I have argued, doing research well necessarily involves reliance on situational judgements, albeit guided by principles. This is particularly true in the case of ethnography. There is no form of transparency that will allow others to see, or to be completely assured, that what is being done conforms to "best practice", in the sense of what it would be best to do in the specific circumstances faced. Pretending that there is some means of doing this, by enforcing procedures, damages ethnographic research.

Any attempt to deal with the ethical dangers associated with research must be proportionate, and should respect the limits of what is possible – rather than simply assuming that transparent accountability via proceduralist regulation is achievable, and that it will eliminate all uncertainty and risk. The risks associated with most social research are very different from, and arguably much less severe than, those involved in testing medical treatments, which is where the pressure for ethical regulation originally arose.[5] Furthermore, non-experimental research, and especially that involving the collection of unstructured data in the field, is much less open to prospective, procedural control than experimental work. Indeed, attempts to achieve this will almost always be counterproductive.

It is also worth emphasising that researchers have never been free to do as they wish, contrary to what often seems to be assumed about the past. Prior to the spread of ethical regulation, they nevertheless operated in situations where legal rules applied; where other agents, notably gatekeepers but also sometimes research participants, had considerable power over the research process; and where there was always the prospect that colleagues would bring what they regarded as unethical behaviour to public attention, resulting in reputational damage for the researcher concerned, at the very least.[6] Any justification put forward for ethical regulation needs to demonstrate that these curbs were, and are, inadequate. It also needs to show that ethical regulation works in minimising, or at least reducing, unethical behaviour on the part of researchers. Yet there is little evidence that it does; indeed, determining this is fraught with difficulties because of the variable judgements that can be made about what is and is not ethical (see Dingwall

2016). These judgements are rarely a matter of the straightforward application of a single principle, and as a result there is considerable scope for reasonable disagreement about what would and would not be ethical. This is precisely why *phrónēsis* is required, and why the attempt to achieve "transparency" is unrealistic, while attempts to achieve it will very often have damaging consequences.[7]

Even if ethnographic research necessarily depends upon *phrónēsis*, this does not rule out the desirability of guidelines, such as the "codes" developed by professional associations. However, rather than laying down injunctions to be followed, these must recognise that ethical considerations – specifically those relating to how researchers deal with the people they study – are multiple and potentially in conflict, and that they are not the only considerations that must be taken into account in doing research. Above all, codes must acknowledge that researchers have an obligation to pursue worthwhile knowledge effectively, and to do this in a way that is *prudent*, for instance, keeping any risk of serious harm to themselves below an acceptable threshold.

The role of *phrónēsis* does not eliminate all the functions of ethics committees, but they should no longer be regulatory bodies determining whether or not research projects can go ahead. As Murphy and Dingwall (2007) argued, "it is time to reclaim research ethics from the bureaucrats" (p. 2231). Instead, ethics committees ought to be fora in which researchers are required to outline and defend their research proposals, or to defend research they have already carried out where this has generated ethical concerns.[8] In this way, ethics committees could play an important role in facilitating the development of *phrónēsis* on the part of researchers, since they would force greater attention to methodological and ethical issues, and expose individual researchers to diverse views about these. At present, the regulatory function of ethics committees seriously inhibits this process, and thereby damages ethnographic research.

Notes

1 Gray is here discussing the philosopher Michael Oakeshott's critique of what he labels "rationalism"; see Oakeshott 1962.
2 There is a parallel between moralism and the religious enthusiasm that Locke and others objected to in the seventeenth century, as part of their defence of political liberalism (Locke 1975: chapter 19).
3 See http://ukrio.org/wp-content/uploads/UKRIO-Code-of-Practice-for-Research.pdf.
4 See http://ec.europa.eu/research/swafs/index.cfm?pg=policy&lib=ethics.
5 Stark (2011: 2 and passim) has argued that, even in the case of medicine, ethical regulation "has served to enable research as much as to restrict it", including some that many would regard as unethical.
6 For examples of cases where colleagues have called one another to account in the context of social research, see Hammersley and Traianou 2012: chapter 1.
7 The case of medical research, and indeed any experimental research that involves treatments that carry with them substantial risks of harm, as well as potential benefit, is different from that of most social research. Here, the potential dangers of ethical regulation may be

outweighed by the risks carried by the research. However, it is important to note that even here regulation cannot deliver transparent accountability, nor does it necessarily prevent harm. Of course, ethical regulation can have beneficial consequences, in terms of prompting researchers to take more account of ethical considerations, to recognise problems that they had overlooked etc. However, these benefits could be gained in other ways.

8 For various other proposals for reform, see Carpenter 2007; Feeley 2007; Hyman 2007; Stark 2007; Marlow and Tolich 2015; van den Hoonaard and Hamilton 2016.

References

ALLEA. 2017. *The European Code of Conduct for Research Integrity* (revised edition). Available at https://ec.europa.eu/research/participants/data/ref/h2020/other/hi/h2020-ethics_code-of-conduct_en.pdf.

Baggini, J. 2018. "How to compare fruit: the limited ambitions of ethical thinking". *Times Literary Supplement* 6008 (May 25): 7–9.

Bok, S. 1978. *Lying: Moral Choice in Public and Private Life*. Hassocks, Sussex: Harvester Press.

Bruun, H.H. 2007. *Science, Values and Politics in Max Weber's Methodology*. Aldershot: Ashgate.

Bulmer, M., ed. 1982. *Social Research Ethics: An Examination of the Merits of Covert Participant Observation*. London: Macmillan.

Calvey, D. 2000. "Getting on the door and staying there: a covert participant observational study of bouncers". In *Danger in the Field: Risk and Ethics in Social Research*, edited by G. Lee-Treweek and S. Linkogle, chapter 3. London: Routledge.

Calvey, D. 2008. "The art and politics of covert research: doing 'situated ethics' in the field". *Sociology* 42(5): 905–918.

Calvey, D. 2017. *Covert Research: The Art, Politics and Ethics of Undercover Fieldwork*. London: Sage.

Carpenter, D. 2007. "Institutional review boards, regulatory incentives, and some modest proposals for reform". *Northwestern University Law Review* 101(2): 723–733. http://scholarship.law.umn.edu/faculty_articles/352.

Coady, C.A.J. 2005. "Preface". *Journal of Applied Philosophy* 22(2): 101–104.

Dancy, J. 2004. *Ethics Without Principles*. Oxford: Oxford University Press.

Delamont, S. and Atkinson, P. 2018. "The ethics of ethnography". In *The Sage Handbook of Qualitative Research Ethics*, edited by R. Iphofen and M. Tolich, 119–132. London: Sage.

Dingwall, R. 2006. "Confronting the anti-democrats: the unethical nature of ethical regulation in social science". Summary of Plenary Address to British Sociological Association Medical Sociology Group Annual Conference, Edinburgh, September. www.academia.edu/1184594/Confronting_the_anti-democrats_The_unethical_nature_of_ethical_regulation_in_social_science.

Dingwall, R. 2008. "The ethical case against ethical regulation in humanities and social science research". *Twenty-First Century Society* [now *Contemporary Social Science*] 3(1): 1–12.

Dingwall, R. 2012. "How did we ever get into this mess? The rise of ethical regulation in the social sciences". In *Ethics in Social Research*, edited by K. Love, 3–25. Bingley: Emerald.

Dingwall, R. 2016. "The social costs of ethics regulation". In *The Ethics Rupture: Exploring Alternatives to Formal Research-Ethics Review*, edited by W.C. van den Hoonaard and A. Hamilton, 25–42. Toronto: University of Toronto Press.

Douglas, J. 1976. *Investigative Social Research*. Beverly Hills, CA: Sage.

Dreyfus, H. and Dreyfus, S. 1986. *Mind Over Machine: The Power of Human Intuition and Expertise in the Era of the Computer*. New York: The Free Press.

Dreyfus, S. 2004. "A five-stage model of the activities involved in teaching skills". *Bulletin of Science, Technology & Society* 24(3): 177–181.

Dunne, J. 1997. *Back to the Rough Ground: Practical Judgment and the Lure of Technique*. Notre Dame, IN: University of Notre Dame Press.

Duster, T., Matza, D. and Wellman, D. 1979. "Fieldwork and the protection of human subjects". *American Sociologist* 14(1): 136–142.

Emmerich, N. 2018. "From *phrónēsis* to Habitus: synderesis and the practice(s) of ethics and social research". In *Virtue Ethics in the Conduct and Governance of Social Science Research* (3rd volume), edited by R. Iphofen, 197–217. London: Emerald, AcSS.

Eraut, M. 1994. *Developing Professional Knowledge and Competence*. London: Falmer Press.

Feeley, M. 2007. "Legality, social research, and the challenge of institutional review boards". *Law & Society Review* 41(4): 757–776.

Gray, J. 2009. *Gray's Anatomy: Selected Writings*. London: Allen Lane.

Haggerty, K. 2004. "Ethics creep: governing social science research in the name of ethics". *Qualitative Sociology* 27(4): 391–414.

Hamburger, P. 2007. "Getting permission". *Northwestern University Law Review* 101(2): 405–492.

Hammersley, M. 2009. "Against the ethicists: on the evils of ethical regulation". *International Journal of Social Research Methodology* 12(3): 211–225.

Hammersley, M. 2018. "Is *phrónēsis* necessarily virtuous?" In *Virtue Ethics in the Conduct and Governance of Social Science Research* (3rd Volume), edited by R. Iphofen, 179–195. London: Emerald, AcSS.

Hammersley, M. and Traianou, A. 2011. "Moralism and research ethics: a Machiavellian perspective". *International Journal of Social Research Methodology* 14(5): 379–390.

Hammersley, M. and Traianou, A. 2012. *Ethics in Qualitative Research*. London: Sage.

Homan, R. 1980. "The ethics of covert methods". *British Journal of Sociology* 31(1): 46–59.

Hyman, D. 2007. "Institutional review boards: is this the least worst we can do?" *Northwestern University Law Review* 101(2): 749–773.

Katz, J. 2007. "Toward a natural history of ethical censorship". *Law & Society Review* 41(4): 797–810.

Krajewski, B. 2011. "The dark side of *phrónēsis*: revisiting the political incompetence of philosophy". *Classica* (Brasil) 24(1/2): 7–21.

Larson, M.S. 1977. *The Rise of Professionalism*. Berkeley, CA: University of California Press.

Leo, R. 1995. "Trial and tribulations: courts, ethnography and the need for evidentiary privilege for academic researchers". *American Sociologist* 26(1): 113–134.

Littrell, B. 1993. "Bureaucratic secrets and adversarial methods of social research". In *A Critique of Contemporary American Sociology*, edited by T. Vaughan, G. Sjoberg and L. Reynolds, 207–231. Dix Hills, NY: General Hall.

Locke, J. 1975 (1689). *An Essay Concerning Human Understanding*, edited by P.H. Nidditch. Oxford: Oxford University Press.

Macfarlane, B. 2009. *Researching with Integrity: The Ethics of Academic Inquiry*. London: Routledge.

MacIntyre, A. 1981. *After Virtue*. London: Duckworth.

Marlow, J. and Tolich, M. 2015. "Shifting from research governance to research ethics: a novel paradigm for ethical review in community-based research". *Research Ethics* 11(4): 178–191.

Montgomery, K. 2006. *How Doctors Think: Clinical Judgment and the Practice of Medicine*. Oxford: Oxford University Press.

Murphy, E. and Dingwall, R. 2007. "Informed consent, anticipatory regulation and ethnographic practice". *Social Science & Medicine* 65(11): 2223–2234.

Oakeshott, M. 1962. *Rationalism in Politics and Other Essays*. London: Methuen.

Pollitt, C. 1990. *Managerialism and the Public Services: The Anglo-American Experience*. Oxford: Blackwell.

Power, M. 1997. *The Audit Society: Rituals of Verification*. Oxford: Oxford University Press.

Pring, R. 2001. "The virtues and vices of an educational researcher". *Journal of Philosophy of Education* 35(3): 407–421.

Roulet, T., Gill, M., Stengers, S. and Gill, D. 2017. "Reconsidering the value of covert research: the role of ambiguous consent in participant observation". *Organizational Research Methods* 20(3): 487–517.

Schrag, Z.M. 2010. *Ethical Imperialism: Institutional Review Boards and the Social Sciences, 1965–2009*. Baltimore, MD: The Johns Hopkins University Press.

Shils, E. 1956. *The Torment of Secrecy*. London: Heinemann.

Shweder, R. 2006. "Protecting human subjects and preserving academic freedom: prospects at the University of Chicago". *American Ethnologist* 33(4): 507–518.

Stark, L. 2011. *Behind Closed Doors: IRBs and the Making of Ethical Research*. Chicago: University of Chicago Press.

Strauss, L. 1987. "Machiavelli". In *History of Political Philosophy* (3rd edition), edited by L. Strauss and J. Cropsey, chapter 11. Chicago: University of Chicago Press.

Traianou, A. 2006. *Understanding Teacher Expertise in Primary Science: A Sociocultural Approach*. Rotterdam: SeNSS.

Traianou, A. 2007. "Ethnography and the perils of the single case: an example from the sociocultural analysis of primary science expertise". *Ethnography and Education* 2(2): 209–220.

Traianou, A. 2014. "The centrality of ethics in qualitative research". In *The Oxford Handbook of Qualitative Research Methods*, edited by P. Leavy, chapter 4. New York: Oxford University Press.

Traianou, A. 2018. "Ethical regulation of social research versus the cultivation of *phrónēsis*". In *Virtue Ethics in the Conduct and Governance of Social Science Research* (3rd volume), edited by R. Iphofen, 163–177. London: Emerald, AcSS.

UKRIO. 2009. Code of Practice for Research: Promoting Good Practice and Preventing Misconduct. http://ukrio.org/wp-content/uploads/UKRIO-Code-of-Practice-for-Research.pdf.

Van den Hoonaard, W.C. 2011. *The Seduction of Ethics: Transforming the Social Sciences*. Toronto: University of Toronto Press.

Van den Hoonaard, W.C. and Hamilton, A., eds. 2016. *The Ethics Rupture: Exploring Alternatives to Formal Research-Ethics Review*. Toronto: University of Toronto Press.

Warwick, D. 1982. "Types of harm in social research". In *Ethical Issues in Social Science Research*, edited by T.L. Beauchamp, chapter 2. Baltimore, MD: Johns Hopkins University Press.

Wieringa, S., Engebretsen, E., Heggen, K. and Greenhalgh, T. 2017. "Has evidence-based medicine ever been modern? A Latour-inspired understanding of a changing EBM". *Journal of Evaluation in Clinical Practice* 23(5): 964–970.

Whitty, G. 2000. "Teacher professionalism in new times". *Journal of InService Education*, 26(2): 281–295.

Chapter 3

Ethical review boards
Constitutions, functions, tensions and blind spots

Dennis Beach and Begoña Vigo Arrazola

Introduction

Ethical appraisal boards (subsequently referred to as ethical review boards) are often argued as being modelled on utilitarian ethical conventions and as operating from a perspective of national political sovereignty that is potentially marginalising and possibly even harmful towards critical qualitative educational research, particularly ethnography (Beach & Eriksson 2010; Busher, Chapter 5, this volume; Dennis 2010, 2018, Chapter 9, this volume; Denzin & Giardina 2007; Flinders 1992; Zachary 2011). These types of assertion have also been identified by, for instance, Farrell (2001) and also Franklin (1995), but as these authors suggest, the legislative responsibility of human rights in research shouldn't be confused with unnecessary bureaucratic intervention (Tobin 1995), for although the work of ethical appraisal can be experienced as intrusive, threatening towards researcher autonomy and professionalism, and unnecessarily bureaucratic (Zachary 2011), using qualitative methods to elicit people's perspectives on their environment is not uncomplicated from the perspectives of human rights, not the least those of young people in school (Morrow 2001). This tension between a notion of imposed bureaucracy and a necessary protection of rights is considered in the present chapter, which tries to bring a balanced critique of the work of ethical review boards into view. It tries to keep sight of possible values but without denying that there are some potentially troubling tensions.

The introduction of ethical review boards

The introduction of ethical review boards in social sciences and humanities research was deemed to be essential to safeguard human rights in research. They began to be introduced into social sciences and humanities fields from roughly the 1990s (Benčin et al. 2015; Zachary 2011) and in education research this was primarily to protect the rights of children (Tobin 1995). At the EU level, they were addressed by the *EU Code of Ethics for Socio-Economic Research*, written as a part of the RESPECT project, as well as in the *Guidance Note for Researchers and Evaluators of Social Sciences and Humanities Research* by the European Commission. They had become part of the landscape of most, though not all, research systems in Europe by the end of that decade (Benčin et al. 2015). However, there were exceptions. In Denmark, for instance, a working group established by the Danish Social Sciences and the Danish Humanities Research in the mid-1990s deemed they were not necessary in these areas (Benčin et al. 2015).

The following points were stressed in the EU statements on research ethics: the need for *upholding human dignity, avoiding harm*; expressing that research involvement was *voluntary*, that *informed consent* had been obtained and that *confidentiality* was guaranteed along with full respect for *cultural differences*. That research projects showed regard for vulnerable participants was also present and these commitments were generally reproduced in national assessment guidelines in partner countries (Benčin et al. 2015; Jacobson et al. 2007). Regard for *disadvantaged* or *underrepresented* individuals and groups or communities and care concerning the publication and *dissemination* of research results were also included.

Emphasis was often placed on the rights and protection of children and vulnerable participants. This was part of traditional conceptualisations of childhood and disability, it seems. Traditionally children were considered to be in need of protection, as not yet adult and as therefore unready to take responsibilities as socially constructive reflective individuals (Prout & James 1997; Tobin 1995), and ethical appraisal was meant to safeguard their rights to protection from harm and to protect their individual integrity (Jacobson et al. 2007). This applied also to other so-called vulnerable participants (Benčin et al. 2015). However, there was a tension here. The rights of children became part of global human rights pronouncements in the United Nations Convention on the Rights of the Child in 1989, and this pronouncement departed from a very different perspective on childhood than one that conceived them as incomplete adults who were always in need of special protection and treatment (James et al. 1998).

Instead of only being described as vulnerable, children were presented in the UN Convention as capable and as deserving respect and recognition as reflective beings who were able to actively and socially own their own world, and instead of objectifying children and childhood researchers were encouraged to work together with children in ways that positioned them as competent and capable of generating their own accounts of everyday experience and responding to the representations of others (Prout & James 1997; Tobin 1995). This applied also regarding people with official disabilities, following the United Nations Convention of Rights of People with Disabilities in 2008, and it has made following a simple list of ethical does and don'ts rather problematic. Children and the disabled are to be treated as fully reflective human subjects who should not be exposed to objectifications that challenge their right to autonomy. It made the use of ethical checklists problematic as they actually undermine this autonomy (Busher, Chapter 5, this volume; Dennis, Chapter 9, this volume).

The present chapter aims to discuss the necessity to develop explicit guidelines for conducting qualitative studies with regard to the researchers' role under these circumstances. It is based on empirical research in Sweden and Spain where research ethics laws have been introduced in the past two decades and it uses empirical materials that comprise four types of data: official documents pertaining to the ethical committees in Europe generally and the two countries of Spain and Sweden in particular, notes from participation on boards and conversations their members, interview material with researchers about the appraisal processes and their experiences of it and previous research connected to research ethics in social sciences and the humanities generally with a consideration in particular for implications for ethnographic research in education (also Beach & Eriksson 2010). We make a call for a view of ethical appraisal in the form of a new partnership that makes good use of the expertise of the members of ethical appraisal boards and develops an already-existing potential with respect to board activities in terms of their pedagogical and advisory function. Sweden and Spain are in focus because of our familiarity with social science and education research and research ethics there, not because they form some kind of special exception or case in relation to ethnographic research and research ethics.

The constitution and activities of ethical review boards

Ethical appraisal committees have been constructed in the two countries with regard to an expressed need of and intention to protect individual human beings in relation to research practices and outcomes, and as a way to help researchers to obtain guarantees that they have done what is needed (and required of them) by law, with regard to upholding respect for human value in their research. They have therefore both a controlling function and a pedagogical function in this respect based on the integrated intellectual labour of two groups of highly informed and aware constituencies; specifically, ethical board members and research teams, both of whom should be strongly committed to ensuring the integrity and safety from harm of human subjects in research projects (Jacobson et al. 2007; Tobin 1995; Zachary 2011). To these ends, the ethical review boards provide the following (Table 3.1).

Education research involving human subjects will normally fall outside of the ethical appraisals acts and will not require an ethical decision by the ethics appraisal boards. Usually an advisory comment is available in these circumstances. This is a decision that is requested by the lead researcher, the project owner based on their own deliberations or, perhaps more often, demands from funders and publishers. It comprises first a formal comment from an ethical appraisals committee that the project does not fall under the ethical appraisals acts and does not need to be assessed in relation to the data acts and ethical principles for good research, but that an assessment and advisory comment has been requested. The ethical review

Table 3.1 Ethical board roles and activities

1 Decisions about the ethical suitability of research based on	2 Informed and guiding comments concerning research practices related to

a   the provision of clear information about research to research subjects
b   data protection laws concerning prolonged safe storage and access to research materials
c   obtaining consent to research from those it involves
d   the processing of sensitive personal data[1]
e   whether research methods risk physically or psychologically influencing the research subjects and whether they constitute an obvious risk of physical or psychological harm
f   that physical or psychological influence or risks have been identified for research subjects and the ways they are to be dealt with are made clear

[1]This is sanctioned in relation to section 13 of the Personal Data Act of 1998 (SFS 1998: 204) in Sweden and by section VII of the Personal Data Act of 1999 (Organic Law 15/1999, 13 December) relating to religion, sexuality and ethnicity in Spain, as well as to personal criminal data acts according to Section 21 of the Personal Data Act (SFS 1998: 204) in Sweden and Section I, Article 7 of the Personal Data Act of 1999 Organic Law 15/1999 in Spain.

boards charge a nominal fee for this appraisal which goes towards administration costs. In Sweden the fee was 500 euro (5000 SEK) at the time of writing the original paper on which the present chapter is based (i.e., spring 2017).

The advisory comment addresses the ethical qualities of the project design and the same legal points that would have needed to be addressed if the application had fallen under the data protection act and the ethics law. The difference is that it is given in the form of comments and recommendations not legal requirements. The recommendations will normally relate to whether storage and access to data are sufficiently well controlled and whether research subjects are sufficiently informed about and able in writing to clearly agree or express dissent to the overall research plan. The common points concern whether:

- information about the project has been communicated clearly and unambiguously to participants in an everyday language concerning the purpose of the research and the methods that will be used
- the consequences and risks that research may cause for research subjects
- the levels of caution that will be taken in the event of any complications
- who the lead researcher is
- that participation is voluntary and that the research subject is always legally entitled to withdraw participation at any time without any kind of sanction
- that consent can be withdrawn with immediate effect but that the data that has been collected may be used in the research
- who the legally responsible officer for data protection and personal information is

Constitution of boards and board members

Ethical review boards in Sweden and Spain are constituted by:

- ten members with scientific (research) expertise in the social sciences and humanities
- an appointed chairperson, often with a law degree and juridical experience
- an elected scientific secretary from among the scientifically qualified board members
- five lay members representing specific interest fields and groups

In Sweden, there is one central and six regional boards, in Lund, Göteborg, Linköping Stockholm, Uppsala and Umeå, respectively. In Spain, the EBs are constituted close to the universities, such as in Barcelona, Madrid, Cádiz, Navarra etc. In partnership projects involving different international partners, project components are assessed by ethical committees that are legally appointed in the countries they will take place in.

The following principles apply with respect to deliberations in both countries. They correspond with the *EU Code of Ethics for Socio-Economic Research* but are based on national not European Law and include:

- giving particular attention as to whether research subjects may for any reason be challenged regarding their capacity to provide informed consent and whether obtaining consent has paid attention to linguistic and cultural differences
- making sure consent has been correctly addressed. Parents or guardians provide informed consent for children who are under fourteen years old but the child must be consulted and their commitment must be respected. Custodians provide consent for people with severe mental challenges
- making sure the research project is led by an appropriately qualified and competent researcher for the research activities
- making sure that participation in the project is expressed as voluntary and that the research shows respect for the participant and her/his rights to protection, care over information access and storage, personal integrity and cultural differences
- making sure data storage, treatment and access meet legal requirements
- considering and assessing whether projects address sensitive questions or contain sensitive data and whether this sensitivity is appropriately respected and responded to

Information to participants is an important point generally (Benčin et al. 2015). It should normally be provided, and informed consent should be gathered personally (*ibid.*). However, next of kin can be contacted as can other representatives, such as a custodian, parent or guardian. Research should not involve a participant who has in any way signaled that they do not wish to take part but research can still be assessed as fulfilling ethical standards in circumstances where informed consent has not been given, if the research can be expected to provide knowledge that isn't possible to obtain if informed consent is asked for (Benčin et al. 2015). This is also possible if the research is expected to be of direct benefit to the research participant and involves minimal risk for injury or discomfort for her/him (*ibid.*).

Some complications of ethical appraisal from the situatedness of ethnographic research

Following the simple guidelines provided by ethical review boards will usually be sufficient for most research projects to pass ethical appraisal (Heath, Hindmarsh & Luff 2010), but as the chapters of Busher and Dennis in this volume also point out (Chapters 5 and 9, respectively), establishing trustful ethical relationships and participation with all research subjects (and on all encounters with them) doesn't stop there. Thus, whilst things like legal and organisational considerations around storage, data access and archiving and preserving identity protection in respect to reporting and dissemination are important legally enforced minimum requirements with regard to a researcher or research group or project's ethical obligations to research subjects, as discussed already in the Introduction, being research-ethical as an education ethnographer really involves more that this (Dennis 2010, 2018; Jacobson et al. 2007). Moreover, although they may be deemed necessary, ethics checklists are not without their problems.

Some of these problems are discussed extensively in earlier chapters in the present book. They have been introduced already there, but also earlier in this chapter, in terms of the tensions between autonomy and objectification brought about by the introduction of ethical appraisal requirements at the same time as new conventions on childhood and the rights of children and people with disabilities have emerged. As Dennis points out (2010, 2018), decisions about what is ethical or not are quintessentially situational and this can't be changed simply by the education ethnographer entering the field legitimised through approvals by ethical review boards, as a hopefully self-aware and reflective researcher, with basically good intentions. The question of what it means to be ethical as an educational ethnographer goes beyond ratifications of the awareness and good intentions of the researcher by ethical appraisals boards, and as Busher also notes in this book (Chapter 5), being ethical as a researcher cannot be isolated from how we contemplate, confront and engage as ethical beings in the world with others, within and during our research, and this is something that is decided in terms of one's holdings and actions towards others as they unfold in practice, not in terms of how they are described and assessed before the fact.

What is ethical is decided in practice then (Dennis 2010), in situated interactions (Busher, Chapter 5, this volume) and on an ongoing basis that cannot be finally decided in advance of research encounters, except in terms of basic minimum requirements and commitments based on descriptions of expressed holdings and anticipated actions towards others (Beach & Eriksson 2010). Thus, what it means to be an ethical ethnographer cannot therefore be fully captured in what can be evaluated by ethical assessment boards (Dennis 2010; Dovemark, Chapter 7, this volume). It has to do with how researchers take responsibility in the practical domain of their research in everyday life and for the entanglements they help to enact and the commitments they are willing to take on in these respects (Benčin et al. 2015; Dennis 2018, Chapter 9, this volume; Zachary 2011).

These things are not easy to predict in advance of the research (Dennis 2010) but this is recognised in guidelines to the ethical review boards in the two countries and in the EU code of ethics as well (Benčin et al. 2015), which also identifies that the course of ethical actions is both situationally forged and guided by first-hand experiences, as well as by commitments to scientific, ideological and political goals, beliefs and practices, and that behaving ethically as an ethnographer is something that has to be crafted from within research projects where claims to truth have become troublingly micro-scoped at the same time as they are also understood in terms of their broader consequences (Beach & Eriksson 2010; Dovemark, Chapter 7, this volume). The research is recognised as open, the researcher is recognised as distinctly fallible and what is ethical is expressed as not fully possible to decide on in advance (Dennis, Chapter 9, this volume; Dovemark, Chapter 7, this volume). It involves "crafting out an ethical stance" through an honest engagement with local communities that incorporates a willingness to respect the values of the other (Dennis 2018) based on an understanding of the actual situation in which the research is being conducted (Busher, Chapter 5, this volume).

What are sought by boards are therefore only certain guarantees in relation to ethical standards that can be measured against a checklist of rights and wrongs and this is also actually recognised in board contexts and in their legal guiding and advisory documents. Ethics are stated there in similar kinds of ways to the statements by Busher, Dennis and Dovemark in this volume, as processual and as requiring both self-regulation and self-reflexivity over the effects or implications of the researcher's presence within, representation of and possible effects on the communities they research (Benčin et al. 2015). This expressed position ironically thus actually somewhat reflects the post-structural position against the modernist notion that "ethical behaviour" can be reduced to a universally applicable codified set of rules. Ethical review boards are critiqued in terms of this but perhaps they are not actually as guilty of modernist impositions as they are suggested to be (Benčin et al. 2015).

This is also clear in relation to the national guidelines to ethical appraisal boards in the two countries we have given most attention to in this chapter, board guidelines recognise that all disciplines are characterised by competing schools of thought, and possibly even by disagreement on fundamental questions of scientific theory, and they recommend therefore that those who are responsible for the assessment of others' work must as a consequence of this be willing to seriously consider arguments and ways of thinking that are asserted by approaches other than their own and ones that currently have national recognition. Moreover, they add, research must be safeguarded against control that interferes with well-founded problems for discussion that are at loggerheads with particular financial, political, social, cultural or religious interests and traditions. These points are picked up in other national guidelines as well (Benčin et al. 2015), as well as in documents such as the CSIC Presidency-commissioned Code of Good Scientific Practices for the integrity and ethical quality of scientific research.

These international concepts do not override national legislation but, according to both sources, ethical appraisals have a recognised role to play in setting and assessing the upkeep of standards of practice without either privileging or excluding competing schools of thought, different theoretical perspectives and approaches or being over-steered by financial, political, social, cultural or religious interests and traditions. This doesn't mean that there aren't problems in these respects; however, nor does it mean that the guidelines and rationales that have been adopted are free from complications (Eckersley 1998). The CSIC Presidency-commissioned Code of Good Scientific Practices for the integrity and ethical quality of scientific research points this out too. On page 7 of that document it is stated that the health, safety or welfare of a community or collaborators should not be compromised and a code of conduct, with rules for handling alleged cases of misconduct, should be in place. However, the Code also recognises that the primary responsibility for handling research misconduct is in the hands of those who employ the researchers and they express that these institutions should have a standing or *ad hoc* committee to deal with any possible cases of misconduct.

Anthropocentrism

Ethical appraisal boards have been broadly constituted in Europe for research in two different domains (Benčin et al. 2015; Zachary 2011). The first concerns medical-related research. The second, and most relevant to this chapter, concerns research in education research, psychological research, social research and the humanities (generally called other research involving human subjects or something similar; Benčin et al. 2015). The expression is specifically "human subjects", which environmentalists, post-humanist researchers and new-materialists consider to be problematic (Dennis 2018; Denzin 2018; Eckersley 1998; Pedersen 2007, 2015; Rosiek 2018), as the planet beyond the school, and the species and lives there, seem to have been unfortunately discounted (Eckersley 1998), despite schools and the people and things within them being connected with the nonhuman world "outside" in a myriad of ways (Pedersen 2007, 2015). There has been a new material turn in relation to the current plight of the planet, they point out, and a critical turn within this material turn, concerning biological, ecological, geological and socioeconomic sustainability, health, justice and welfare in a world in the grip of corporate greed and global capitalism. This turn can be read as a reaction to the discursive turn initiated by the crisis of representation and its consequences in terms of an eclipse of materialist reason (Rosiek 2018; Yusoff 2017) and it has clear implications for how research ethics might be considered and assessed (Denzin 2018; Dovemark, Chapter 7, this volume; Pedersen 2007, 2015).

The new-materialist and post-humanist philosophers like Rosiek (2018), critical educational researchers like Pedersen (2007, 2015) and critical environmentalists and geographers like Eckersley (1998) and Yusoff (2017) raise some important points here for research ethics. As they point out, the material destratifications of marine, mineral and chemical flows of carbon and nitrogen are returning in accumulative modalities of pollution, toxicity and climate change that reconfigure the possibilities of life on the planet for humans and other species, yet these essentially human (anthropocenic) matters are generally placed outside the conventional framing of human and social science research as a missing ethical substratum.

As Yussof (2017) writes, everything from McDonalds to Walmart chains – and schools too, of course – and not only the academies that are sponsored by these corporate giants, are part of interlocking geosocial architectures and the organisation of the material structures of space and its temporal patterning under global capitalism that are also rapidly de- and re-stratifying social, economic and mineral practices, and rearranging the global dynamics of human settlement through capitalist exploitation and its regular shifting of material production. Global capitalism and capitalists have taken the politics of the bio- and geospheres as their dominion and have by this created a new rendering of time, subjectivity and agency that announces both a break in and consolidation of modernity's temporal arc (Harvey 2010). Yet whilst this new form of geopolitics is emerging the geological realm as a quality of materiality is not yet a feature of the official ethical appraisal agenda in human and social science (including education) research (Benčin et al. 2015; Pedersen 2015). It is an arena that has been rendered invisible and contractually mute in these respects, as a blind spot on the ethical map that needs to be reconsidered and readdressed in human and non-human planetary interests and survival (Eckersley 1998; Pedersen 2015).

As described in other chapters, introduced as Table 1.3 in Chapter 1 of this volume, Flinders (1992: 113) provided an overview to describe how different ways of thinking related to alternative conceptions of research ethics can be represented. There were four different forms of thinking ethically about human science research. The fourth position, the ecological, was considered, but Table 1.3 was primarily constructed in terms of a hybrid rationality that stretched across three philosophical positions (the utilitarian, the deontological and the relational), and where the ecological domain was principally in fact exclusively defined in terms of its human characteristics and relations. In this act of dominion, post-humanist and new-material ontologies were left outside the domain of ethical thinking even in this representation.

This can, of course, as Rosiek (2018) points out, be quite challenging for the future (wellbeing) of our planet and global sustainability (Eckersley 1998). Like the ecological position, the post-humanist perspective recognises that much of what we do as ethnographic researchers has to be considered unpredictable (Dovemark, Chapter 7, this volume); not the least in terms of its long-term effects (*ibid.*) and that because of this we have to be concerned that places like the schools and classrooms we do our research in are environments that are filled with lives and characterised by communication forms which connect people and things with the world beyond their four walls in ways that we often actually know very little about (*ibid.*; Busher, Chapter 5, this volume, Dennis, Chapter 9, this volume). However, post-humanism and new-materialist ontologies also extend conventional ethical considerations by expanding the circle of moral concern and our understandings of subjectivity/ies (Rosiek 2018) by also including other species and perspectives than the straightforwardly human in its considerations. These sorts of principles inform a mode of ethical regulation that seems quite different to the conventional ways in which many qualitative researchers approach their work in ethical terms (Denzin & Giardina 2007; Hammersley & Traianou 2014).

Denzin and Giardina (2007) speak in this respect about more than just moving beyond the deception-based, utilitarian thinking. They also critique a move to qualitative research that failed to connect with post-qualitative and post-humanist ethics and failed to recognise that emancipatory (critical) social scientific ethnography has a different ontology to mainstream liberal research with different aims and knowledge interests, and that this is important to what is thought of and practised as ethical research and what isn't (Dovemark, Chapter 7, this volume). Critical ethnographers, for instance, will deliberately engage with research subjects in consciousness-raising projects that are intended to change their considerations of social and material political and power relations and the capabilities that are developed to allow and motivate people to engage politically with their circumstances towards social transformation (Mendes 1999). They recognise that (global) capitalism, as Marx's well-known pyramid model identified a century-and-a-half ago, has not only plagued humans in the search for profit, it has also created innumerable planetary problems for which we do not yet have answers, but that have serious consequences for planetary futures. In this way this research falls into the category of using methods that involve some kind of effects on human subjects, including physical and psychological influence, and that may even potentially induce some serious risks. It would fall under the ethical appraisal act but as a vision of research that enables and promotes justice, community, diversity, civic discourse and caring.

This kind of research likens that proposed by Lincoln (1995). It is described as transformative by Mertens, Holmes and Harris (2009) and highlights once again the need and value of situated knowledge as expressed in other chapters of the book, such as those by Busher (Chapter 5), Dennis (Chapter 9) and Dovemark (Chapter 7), respectively. What is ethical in these circumstances is mediated by the functioning of schools, the professionalism of teachers and the involvement of community members. The meaning of ethics becomes related to transformations in practices in educational institutions and to the experiences of those involved in them and the consequences and effects of these experiences.

The ethical stance here is twofold. First, concerning the research itself, it is ethical to share the analysis and interpretation of the collated information with the research subjects just as it is also ethical to take into account participants' opinions on researchers' interpretation of their reality. Second, concerning the research subjects, it is ethical to address research contributions during the process as well as at the end of it, and in terms of action consequences where subjects and researchers develop collaborative, public, pedagogical relationships (Dovemark, Chapter 7, this volume). Participants are not asked to submit to specific procedures or treatment conditions from this research perspective. Researchers and research subjects work carefully together to produce sustainable and mutually worthwhile change in the world (Denzin & Giardina 2007) and they can make use of experts in the field of research ethics in the process to help recover the moral values that may have been excluded by the rational Enlightenment science project and the extension of its ethical epistemologies (Hammersley & Traianou 2014) that privilege human subjectivities and the sensibilities and interests of the dominant class through the cooption and active support of the bourgeoisie. This isn't only an issue of how humans treat animals in research and education (Pedersen 2007). Horrendous though this is, research and development projects are being legislated today (such as fracking, for instance) that are anticipated (not just suspected) to create grave hazards for geological structures and geological and biological permanence and the common human interest has been taken prisoner, malformed and misused in this process. If this isn't an issue for human and social science research ethics, then what is? (Denzin 2018; Denzin & Giardina 2007; Pedersen 2015.)

Concluding remarks

Setting up prescriptive ethics for ethnographic research in advance of concrete, entangled encounters in ethnographic research with reflective and aware human subjects is somewhat problematic, but in present global conditions, and contrary to the way ethical practices and their assessments are currently inscribed (following, for instance, current EU and various national prescriptions; Benčin et al. 2015), it is done, and it is done in relation to a pretense about the protection of the human subject and humans first as operationalised through bourgeois values (Dennis 2018; Pedersen 2015). This can be considered to be a problem, as in this way ethical review boards (and education and education research perhaps more substantially and generally) actually fail to foreground one of the most important reasons concerning why we educate young people in the first place, and in what (Tobin 1995). That is, in terms of how to be and act as a moral subject in the interests of justice, survival and wellbeing and in terms of the relationships we form with the world and all things in it, including not only other species but also what has been classified as inanimate material (Rosiek 2018; Yusoff 2017). To do less is to disrespect the duty of care in research for research participants and subjects (Dovemark, Chapter 7, this volume), including not only other human beings (Busher, Chapter 5, this volume), but also animals, the environment and cultural objects (Eckersley 1998; Pedersen 2007, 2015).

Ethical review boards and guidelines, such as those of the EU (Benčin et al. 2015) can be accused of not doing this, but of instead asserting ethical standards as prescriptions that actually close the door on the question of ethical practices in ways that reify and predetermine ethical holdings in favour of humans, above planetary needs (Pedersen 2007, 2015). However, ethical review boards don't only ratify the safeguards provided to human subjects by law; they also give advice connected to further possibilities that can develop, including giving attention to cross-species communication where this might be relevant, such as by thinking about the animals that might be present in schools (physically and symbolically) and how the way we act on the world and represent those actions can operate to condition subjectivity, by being proximate not only to concepts of human sub-jectivities as developed in the mirror images of the bourgeoisie (its mental states, its body, its meanings etc.) but also considering life from other perspectives and values inherent in "other" subjects and the lives of non-subjective things – i.e., a totality of planetary (and production) relations.

The main activities (in volume at least) of ethical appraisals boards can make important and informed interventions here. These main actions are the giving of good advice, not the making of legally sanctioned decisions. These recommen-dations are non-prescriptive, but they are generally very well informed. Board members are given induction courses when joining the boards and courses at regular intervals. The content of these courses is kept fully up to date and will include input concerning developments in moral philosophy, practical philosophy and the post-humanist critique of ethical appraisals and their reinforcement of the concept of dominion. They are therefore also fully aware that they cannot set up *any* prescriptive ethics for ethnographers and how they will behave in the research field in advance of their concrete, entangled encounters there, which board mem-bers also point out when asked about this. Nor do they try to do so – which they likewise point out when given the chance – at least not beyond legally demanded care-full practices such as those stipulated in ethical guidelines for practice and ethical appraisal questionnaires (Benčin et al. 2015).

Board members are in this sense constantly updated reflective professionals in relation to key issues of research ethics, who can and do fulfil a valuable pedagogi-cal and advisory role as opposed to forming (only) a bureaucratic encumbrance or a legislative function. The majority of them are also researchers in the social and human sciences who are fully cognisant with advanced concepts there, such as the concept of dominion and how it can transform agriculture into agribusiness with its attendant uses of monocultural farming, genetic modification and ubiquitous herbi- and pesticides.

Dominion props up the humanist fantasy that we are a separate (and special) species and it has authorised the slaughter of billions of animals in the deformed (and deforming/alienating) interest not of putting food on the table of the starving populations, but of capitalist corporate global profit. Ethical board members and their activities may thus inadvertently support the global fantasy of a good life for all. But although they appear to be tied to a viewpoint on the world that situates everything in relation to humans and their defined needs and values as private economic individuals, they are in fact officially instructed and legislated to not do this, as pointed out in earlier pages. Quite the opposite to taking the one dominant side of things from one theoretical perspective, documents like the *EU Code of Ethics for Socio-Economic Research* from the RESPECT project and the *Guidance Note for Researchers and Evaluators of Social Sciences and Humanities Research* by the European Commission (also Benčin et al. 2015) and in documents such as the CSIC Presidency-commissioned Code of Good Scientific Practices for the integrity and ethical quality of scientific research point out instead that research must be safeguarded against control that interferes with well-founded problems for discussion and that are at loggerheads with particular financial, political, social, cultural or religious interests and traditions.

There is then, perhaps as ever, a reality, and an illusion of reality that promotes the hegemony of the dominant class interest and stands in the way of true reason. This is a problem that critical research pursues (Dovemark, Chapter 7, this volume) but it is also a project that the object-oriented ontologies of new materialism and post-humanism pursue as well (Pedersen 2015). And as these researchers point out, it seems reasonable to ask, therefore, what such an ontology might do if it was applied more overtly in relation to the pedagogical and advisory work of ethical appraisal boards. These boards do not preclude the use of such a perspective. What they try to ensure is that regardless of the chosen ontology, research participants and their rights and integrity are considered, and their involvement is safeguarded in particular legally ratified ways with respect to current law and order – which, of course, given the capitalist manipulation of (and degree control over) the law may be a problem – and so far this hasn't demanded that critical or new materialist or post-humanist researchers abandon their ontology or change the aims of their research. The ethics laws in European countries only require that researchers signal a consideration of the rights and values of other people by following specifications for action that are legally required and demonstrating how they have given forethought to possible developments in the research that could lead to harm or the commitment of indiscretions towards others. Ethical review boards are not radically incapable of thinking realities beyond human dominion, nor does their remit tie strictly only onto a particular scientific perspective. But boards are charged with assuring that researchers follow the law, and that they are aware of and respect the rights and security of the human subjects who become involved or implicated in their scientific research.

This is a strength and a weakness. It is a strength in terms of the openness that is expressed but it is ethically insufficient to continue to write about the world and ethical behaviour primarily (and more or less even *only*) in terms of what it means for us humans (particularly as a general category or species) without considering us as part of a planetary whole who are tied to the planet in particular ways through particular and individually different (and differentially constructed political, economic and ecological) relations of interest, control, exploitation and care (Pedersen 2015). Humans are not the same in these respects (for instance, from the North or the South, from the political Right or the Left and from dominated or dominant races, ethnicities and subjectivities)! Humans, ticks, slime moulds and rocks are all objects, capable of constituting uniquely irreducible ecological relations (Pedersen 2015) but the ethical transgressions that are committed in the formation and exploitation of bio-capital and the absorption of education into the Animal-Industrial Complex are not initiated by and benefitted from equally by all of us. This could be factored into the considerations of ethical review boards as a matter of jurisdiction but as yet this doesn't happen (Benčin et al. 2015). Instead, as Pedersen (2007, 2015) points out, education, education research and its ethical epistemologies normalises the capitalisation of meat, dairy and other animal-derived products in school canteens to form subjectivities through subtle manipulations of emotion that allow human-animal relations to be constituted and normalised in terms of parasitic modes of production and consumption. At present, regulating against this kind of exploitation is considered to be outside the domain of ethical deliberation in human and social (including education) research. It is perhaps time, though, that such regimes of thought take a rightful place in tables such as that assembled by David Flinders in 1992 as well as in other similar tables from other sources that are shown in other chapters in the present book.

References

Beach, D. and Eriksson, A. 2010. "The relationship between ethical positions and methodological approaches: A Scandinavian perspective". *Ethnography and Education* 5(2): 129–142.

Benčin, R., Šumič-Riha, J. and Riha, R. 2015. *Ethics Assessment in Different Fields: Humanities.* Annex 2.e. Ethical Assessment of Research and Innovation: A Comparative Analysis of Practices and Institutions in the EU and selected other countries, Deliverable 1.1, *Stakeholders Acting Together on the Ethical Impact Assessment of Research and Innovation* (SATORI). Brussels: European Commission's Seventh Framework Programme (FP7/2007-2013: grant 612231).

Dennis, B. 2010. "Ethical dilemmas in the field: The complex nature of doing education ethnography". *Ethnography and Education* 5(2): 123–127.

Dennis, B. 2018. "Tales of working without/against a compass: Rethinking ethical dilemmas in educational ethnography". In *The Wiley Handbook of Ethnography of Education*, edited by D. Beach, C. Bagley and S. Marques da Silva, 51–70. New York and London: Wiley.

Denzin, N. 2018. "Staging resistance: Theatres of the oppressed". In *The Wiley Handbook of Ethnography of Education*, edited by D. Beach, C. Bagley and S. Marques da Silva, 375–402. New York and London: Wiley.

Denzin, N. and Giardina, M.D. 2007. "Introduction: Ethical futures in qualitative research". In *Ethical Futures in Qualitative Research: Decolonizing the Politics of Knowledge*, edited by N. Denzin and M.D. Giardina, 9–44. Walnut Creek, CA: Left Coast Press.

Eckersley, R. 1998. "Beyond human racism". *Environmental Values* 7(2): 165–182.

Farrell, A. 2001. "Legislative responsibility for child protection and human rights in Queensland". *Australia and New Zealand Journal of Law and Education* 6(1 and 2): 15–24.

Flinders, D. 1992. "In search of ethical guidance: Constructing a basis for dialogue". *International Journal of Qualitative Studies in Education* 5(2): 101–115.

Franklin, B. 1995. *Handbook of Children's Rights: Comparative Policy and Practice*. London: Routledge.

Hammersley, M. and Traianou, A. 2014. "An alternative ethics? Justice and care as guiding principles for qualitative research". *Sociological Research Online* 19(3): 24.

Harvey, D. 2010. "The right to the city: From capital surplus to accumulation by dispossession". In *Accumulation by Dispossession*, edited by S. Banerjee-Guha, 23–53, New Delhi: Sage.

Heath, C., Hindmarsh, J. and Luff, P. 2010. *Video Analysis and Qualitative Research*. Thousand Oaks, CA: Sage.

Jacobson, N., Gewurtz, R. and Haydon, E. 2007. "Ethical review of interpretive research: Problems and solutions". *IRB: Ethics & Human Research* 29(5): 1–8.

James, A., Jenks, C. and Prout, A. 1998. *Theorising Childhood*. Polity Press: Cambridge.

Lincoln, Y.S. 1995. "Emerging criteria for quality in qualitative and interpretive inquiry". *Qualitative Inquiry* 1(3): 275–289.

Mendes, P. 1999. "Marxist and feminist critiques of child protection". *Children Australia* 24(2): 27–31.

Mertens, D., Holmes, H. and Harris, R. 2009. "Transformative research and ethics". In *Handbook of Social Research Ethics*, edited by D. Mertens and P. Ginsberg, chapter 6. Thousand Oaks, CA: Sage.

Morrow, V. 2001. "Using qualitative methods to elicit young people's perspectives on their environment: Some ideas for community health initiatives". *Health Education Research Theory Practice* 16(3): 255–268.

Pedersen, H. 2007. *The School and the Animal Other: An Ethnography of Human–Animal Relations in Education*. Doctoral thesis. Göteborg: Acta Universitatis Gothoburgensis.

Pedersen, H. 2015. *Education and Posthumanism*. Stockholm: Stockholm University Press.

Prout, A. and James, A. 1997. "A new paradigm for the sociology of childhood? Provenance, promise and problems". In *Constructing and Reconstructing Childhood: Contemporary Issues in the Sociological Study of Childhood*, 2nd edn, edited by A. James and A. Prout, chapter 1. Falmer Press: London.

Rajander, S. 2010. *School and Choice: An Ethnography of a Primary School with Bilingual Classes*. Doctoral thesis. Helsinki: University of Helsinki. Available at: https://helda.helsinki.fi/handle/10138/19728.

Rosiek, J. 2018. "Agential realism and educational ethnography: Guidance for application from Karen Barad's new materialism and Charles Sanders Peirce's material semiotics". In *The Wiley Handbook of Ethnography of Education*, edited by D. Beach, C. Bagley and S. Marques da Silva, 403–422. New York and London: Wiley.

Tobin, J. 1995. "Post-structural research in early childhood education". In *Qualitative Research in Early Childhood Settings*, edited by J. Hatch Praeger, 223–240. Westport, CT: Praeger.

Yusoff, K. 2017. "Epochal aesthetics: Affectual infrastructures of the anthropocene". www.e-flux.com/architecture/accumulation/121847/epochal-aesthetics-affectual-infrastructures-of-the-anthropocene/.

Zachary M. 2011. "The case against ethics review in the social sciences". *Research Ethics* 7(4): 120–131.

Part II

Applying ethics in the field

Chapter 4

Ethics and access when consent must come first

Consequences of formalised research ethics for ethnographic research in schools

Ingrid Smette

Introduction

Schools as fieldwork sites are tempting because they appear to provide easy access to a field. The researcher has permission to be in the place of study, and those studied are obliged to be there – teachers through their work contracts and children through compulsory school attendance. Yet the compulsory attendance of actors in schools is also a challenge, particularly because schools involve minors who may not themselves consent to participating in the research.

In this chapter, I discuss the ethical considerations and, embedded in these, the methodological challenges involved in doing participant observation in an institutional setting where not everyone has consented to participation in the research. More specifically, I focus on the implications of having to obtain consent first – before the onset of the study. I also discuss the ethical and methodological challenges encountered when doing research in schools and classrooms when not everyone participates – what I will define as partially participating collectives.

A main purpose of this discussion is to contribute to a now longstanding but still ongoing debate about the conditions for participant observation in a society with strong formal regulation of participation in research. Implicit in these debates is a distinction between Silverman's (2003) notion of everyday ethics and what Strathern (2000b) calls formalised ethics. Based on her own experiences as an ethnographic researcher, Silverman develops the notion of "everyday ethics", which she defines as the ethical considerations involved in building field relationships.

> Everyday ethics is about crafting a persona and identity that will mutually engage both the researcher and the people, without doing damage to either. Then, it is about the continual need for choices, each day. It is about ambiguity, conflicting interests, fine lines, judgement calls and, therefore, about awkward decisions. This means that every research site is different, as is the personal style which every anthropologist brings to the field.
>
> (Silverman 2003: 127–128)

Silverman (2003) describes the principles of everyday ethics as a chain of connected elements that start with access, thus illustrating how methodological and ethical issues are closely connected in ethnographic research methods. Access usually means achieving some kind of acceptance in the community being studied, which then facilitates inclusion in people's lives and thereby access to the practices and meanings of interest to the fieldworker. Such acceptance relies on continuous negotiations of trust. According to Silverman, trust grants the anthropologist at least *some* kind of membership in the community being studied and can be maintained only if the anthropologist acts towards community members in accordance with the community's expectations. As long as the anthropologist is open about his or her objectives, the research subjects' trust in the anthropologist is regarded as a practical demonstration of consent.

In regimes of formalised ethics, consent is expressed at a different stage of the research process; participants are asked to give their consent after receiving standardised information about the study but before the start of the research itself. The emphasis on institutional procedures, for instance, regarding collection and protecting personal data, suggests that building trust in research institutions and research institutions generally is at the forefront. This distinguishes formalised ethics from everyday ethics describes by Silverman, where participants' trust in the individual researcher is highlighted.

For consent to be valid, it must be informed – that is, knowledgeable, voluntary and exercised by persons competent to consent (Fluehr-Lobban 2003b). Whereas the logic of everyday ethics would imply that consent is demonstrated through people's continuous engagement in their relationship with the researcher, an important principle of formalised ethics is that researchers must be able to document that consent is informed. With the implementation of the new EU regulation on data protection (the General Data Protection Regulation, GDPR) put in place in the EU from 2018, the requirement on researchers to produce evidence of research participants' informed consent is strengthened, thus reinforcing the formalisation of consent procedures.

What are the consequences of these changes for ethnography and, more particularly, participant observation in institutional settings in the future? Anthropologists' position on these matters diverge; some argue that ethical guidelines and state regulations will renew and improve anthropological practice (Fluehr-Lobban 2003a); others oppose regulations that could limit academic freedom and contribute to defining the relationship between researcher and research subjects in ways that presuppose opposing rather than joint interests (Lederman 2006).

One focus in this debate has been on the practical hindrances that formalised ethics entail for the researchers. Ethnographers and other qualitative researchers working in healthcare settings have described how differences between biomedical and social scientific research ethics make such hindrances very tangible. One aspect is the notion of research subjects' vulnerability. Understanding that research subjects are inherently vulnerable, which is the convention in biomedical research ethics, can lead ethics boards to estimate the level of risk of harm as higher and research participants as less-capable of providing consent than if vulnerability was understood differently (Øye, Bjelland & Skorpen 2007).

Another hindrance highlighted by researchers working in healthcare institutions is the requirement to obtain consent from everyone in the setting before the onset of the study. One argument is that this requirement reveals a lack of understanding of the process and social relationships of fieldwork and their importance for the production of knowledge (Mapedzahama & Dune 2017) and that it makes it impossible to conduct participant observation, at least as anthropologists know it in many institutional settings (Øye & Bjelland 2012). Pollock (2012) therefore argues that qualitative studies in healthcare settings need to be evaluated within a different set of criteria than biomedical standards and by reviewers who have a proper understanding of qualitative methodologies

Marilyn Strathern (2000a, 2000b) offers a more radical critique of formalised ethics in the sense that she addresses not so much the practical hindrances it causes, but the premises on which this ethics is based. More specifically, Strathern argues against the definition of anthropological research as "research on human subjects"; for ethnographers, Strathern argues, "Human subjects . . . are not necessarily the subject of the research: That subject is the manifold products of people's interactions" (Strathern 2000a: 294). It follows perhaps from Strathern's position that seeking predictive consent in institutional settings is superfluous, because the ethnographer is not studying individuals and is not interested in personal data about these individuals. However, is it possible to ignore some regulations aimed at protecting privacy under the auspices of studying social interaction, not individual human subjects? Or would this entail compromising the rights of the individuals within the schools *not* to participate in research?

In this chapter, I propose steps to move beyond the tendency to posit formalised ethics and everyday ethics as entirely separate and opposing approaches to ethics, and instead to regard them as connected dimensions of a research process. I also argue that anthropologists could make their engagement with formalised ethics an object of analysis, rather than briefly note this part of the research process as a nuisance in our writings. When researchers omit descriptions of the process of obtaining consent, they also miss out on the opportunity to reflect on how people's decision to participate, or not to participate, may reveal their relationships with institutions and different categories of people.

This chapter, therefore, begins with an unconventionally detailed description of the various steps I took to obtain formal access to schools and pupils during my own PhD research, an ethnographic study of community and boundary drawing among pupils and teachers in two secondary schools in Oslo, Norway (Smette 2015). I then continue with reflections on my approach to conducting participant observation in collectives in which not everyone participates. I also reflect on how parents' consent can be regarded as an expression of their relationship with the schools. Finally, in the discussion and conclusion, I discuss implications of formalised ethics for ethnographic research in schools and propose ways forward.

Reporting for privacy protection

In Norway, ethics reviews of research projects are not carried out at the level of the individual institution but handled by national institutions. The National Committee for Research Ethics in the Social Sciences and the Humanities (NESH) develops guidelines, offers advice to researchers and investigates cases of suspected misconduct in research projects. If a project involves health issues, approval must be obtained from the Regional Ethics Committee (REK). In practice, most ethnographic research projects are reviewed with regard to questions of obtaining and storing personal data. The Data Protection Official for Research (*Personvernombudet for forskning*), hereafter NSD, is appointed as a partner of the Norwegian Data Protection Authority for assessing whether a project is in accordance with statutory data privacy requirements. NSD, on behalf of the Data Protection Authority, either recommends the project or forwards it to the Data Protection Authority for final license (*konsesjon*) and approval or to the Regional Ethics Committee if the project involves health issues.

A few months before the school year was to start, I filed my project with NSD by filling out an electronic form. In this form, I described the "sample" and "process of recruitment" in brief and formal terms; I would select two lower-secondary schools and send requests for participation to the headmaster; the sample would be the tenth-grade pupils in these schools. The description of the sample is required in order for NSD to determine whether written consent from participants or from their parents or guardians is needed. In ethics guidelines for research in Norway, children and young people are regarded as capable of consenting to participation in research from the age of thirteen to fourteen years. The rationale is that children from this age on are "cognitively capable" of understanding the implications of the research and are therefore able to make decisions about participation (Backe-Hansen 2009).

The notion of informed consent triggers specific requirements regarding information that must be provided in information letters. In the notification to NSD, I indicated that I would give written information to parents and pupils in separate information letters. I drafted information letters that the case officer read and corrected. In my letter to the parents I had to explain that I would be talking to pupils about their family background and their parents' views on education. I also had to include information about anonymity and confidentiality, the institution responsible for the project, how the data would be stored and when the sound recordings would be destroyed.

From e-mail and telephone discussions with the NSD case officer, it soon became clear that I would need written consent from parents or guardians because some of the pupils would be younger than sixteen and the project would involve "sensitive personal data".[1] After a few exchanges with the case officer about the information letters, the process was completed and I received an official "recommendation" (*tilråding*) for the project on the condition that it was carried out in accordance with the guidelines.

Participant observation in partially participating collectives

Øye and Bjelland (2012) point to the twofold problem of the requirement to define beforehand the sample and recruitment procedures to be used in the research and the challenges this requirement poses for ethnographic fieldwork, which is unpredictable and emergent. As soon as I began the process of collecting consent forms from the pupils, this was the very concern I experienced: was it going to be possible for me to conduct participant observation in classrooms?

In both schools, the teachers helped me distribute and collect the consent forms. The practical reason was, of course, that they regularly distributed and collected such forms; they had routines for keeping track of who had not yet handed in their form, and they knew which pupils they would have to remind several times. Also, the question of who would make the initial contact with potential informants was on the form that I filled in when reporting the project to NSD. The rationale behind this question is to establish whether "undue pressure" can be put on individuals to participate. If someone other than the researcher takes care of recruiting participants, it is reasonable to presume that there will be no such pressure. Interesting to note here is that the traditional anthropological way of gaining access to and consent from research subjects, through convincing and demonstrating trustworthiness, would easily be regarded as undue pressure within this context. This is especially true in situations where the research subjects are minors or where an assumption of an asymmetric power relationship between the research subject and researcher exists.

At the first school, Woodside, I introduced the project and myself on the opening day of the school year, and the teachers distributed and began collecting the forms over the intervening two weeks before I actually began the fieldwork. When I returned to Woodside two weeks later, I liberated the teachers from the task of following up consent collection and reminded the pupils who had not yet returned the form to do so if they wanted to participate. When the process was completed, sixty-three of the school's seventy-three tenth-graders had consented to participation.

Whereas I did not consider the number of non-participating pupils at Woodside a problem for my fieldwork, the situation at the other school, Lakeside, gave rise to concern. Less than a week before I was to start at Lakeside, my contact person told me that of the sixty-two tenth-graders at the school, thirteen were not going to participate and ten had not yet responded. I found this news distressing. Confronting the prospect that more than a third of the pupils might not participate, I feared that participant observation in the classroom would be ethically and methodically problematic. My concern was reinforced when I met the team of tenth-grade teachers, which was around the time when participation numbers were most uncertain. One of the teachers raised the question of whether it would be right to observe classroom sessions when a large number of pupils had not agreed to participate. I responded that I felt very uncertain and would discuss the matter with my colleagues and supervisors.

When, in the end, forty-nine of the tenth-graders at Lakeside consented to participation, I decided that I could conduct fieldwork in a manner that would not compromise the non-participating pupils. I would, for instance, refrain from observation in groups that included many of the pupils who were not participating in my study. As I had done at Woodside, I began to approach those pupils who had not consented to confirm that I was aware of their non-participation. However, contrary to all but one non-consent decision at Woodside, most of the decisions to decline participation at Lakeside were made by the parents. Because I felt that some of these pupils, girls in particular, were embarrassed when I approached them about this, I simply stopped doing it.

My process of collecting consent forms from the pupils also revealed that in some situations decisions about participation were actually taken collectively, that is, by pupils who were taking others' decisions into consideration when making their own. An illustration of this occurred as I, during the first weeks of fieldwork, was trying to collect the final consent forms from pupils who had not yet returned them. I was moving quietly around one of the classrooms while the pupils were working individually, trying to locate those pupils who had already indicated that they did not wish to participate in my study or had not yet responded. I found one of the boys who had not yet responded and asked him if he had thought about participating or needed a new form. As I approached him, he seemed to decide, as if on impulse, that he did not want to participate. I was unaware that some of the boys around him were his friends. As they became aware of our exchange, three or four of them decided that they did not want to participate either, although I had already received consent forms from some of them. When I later learned that these boys were all low-achievers and were perceived as "problem kids" by the teachers, I realised that what had happened was probably partly a result of my project coming across as being part of school. The situation illustrates, of course, the general problem of gaining consent at the very beginning of the research, but also how the notion of individual, informed consent as necessarily an autonomous decision may be problematic.

Consent and family–school relationships

In research projects involving pupils but requiring parental consent, the family and the school are equally important contexts for research participants' decision to participate – or not. The process of obtaining consent can thus be revealing of pupils as well as parents' relationship with school in its own right. In the context of my study, this process also provided insights into how children could play very different roles in giving consent in different families.

At Woodside, most of the parents consented readily to their child's participation, and the collection of consent forms was completed quite quickly. In all but two cases of non-consent, it was the pupils themselves who decided that they did not want to participate. In addition to the group of boys who refused on grounds that I believe had to do with the project's association with school, as described in the previous paragraph, two high-achieving boys also said no. I met the mother of one of these boys by coincidence, and she explained that her son had not wanted to participate because he believed it would take up too much time in his busy schedule. The mother apologised for her son's non-participation, emphasising that she had tried to convince him, but to no avail.

To my knowledge, in only two cases did parents at Woodside refuse consent. In one case, I learnt from the teachers that the parents, highly educated, did not approve of this kind of research. The other case involved a girl who had recently moved to Woodside from a reception class for immigrants and whose parents, again according to the teacher, did not speak Norwegian and were probably unsure of what the research entailed. The girl left Woodside soon after I began my fieldwork, and I therefore did nothing further to recruit her.

That Woodside parents stressed their child's ownership of the decision not to participate while Lakeside parents appeared to make that decision for their child may be related to different conceptions of young people's autonomy. In my conversation with the Woodside mother whose son was not participating, she demonstrated an understanding that the decision was really his. In respecting her son's refusal to participate, she was making visible her own respect for his autonomy, yet confirming her own positive relationship with the school (and research).

At Lakeside, most of the non-participating pupils were first-generation immigrants. The teachers informed me that the parents of these girls usually responded negatively to similar requests. The parents of the Lakeside girls seemed to have a different understanding of who was responsible for making decisions in such matters: the parents, rather than the young people themselves. They emphasised the autonomy of the family as the unit of decision-making in such matters.

A phone call from a Lakeside parent, however, suggested that perhaps more was behind parental decisions about participation than just a different understanding of autonomy. The father of a boy of minority background had received the information letter, which included my phone number and an encouragement to call if they had questions about the project. The conversation I had with the father was very short. He asked me whether the project would involve an educational benefit; would it, for instance, provide his child with any extra assistance or learning resources? I informed him that the project was not going to provide such resources, whereupon he thanked me for this information and said it confirmed his decision that he did not want his child to participate.

It is clear that making use of the school's established channels for communicating with parents is effective for obtaining consent from many parents. Part of the reason for the effectiveness is that some parents may respond positively to requests to research participation more or less out of habit, as they would with other requests coming from school. If parents feel obliged to participate in order to be regarded as "positive parents" by the teachers, this could undermine the principle of voluntary participation. Similarly, parents may fear that not participating in a research project that takes place at school can have negative consequences for their child – even when the information letter assures that this will not be the case.

Therefore, in order to secure voluntary and informed consent, researchers need to be aware of the possibility that parents may not be able to distinguish between the interests of the researcher and the interests of schools and teachers. In some cases, it would be better to approach parents and pupils through other channels than those made available by the school, both to secure voluntary participation, but also to be in a better position to negotiate the participation of pupils and parents with a troubled relationship with school.

Writing about partially participating collectives

Even after I decided to conduct the observations, despite that some pupils did not participate, many practical and ethical dilemmas remained. One challenge was how to represent my observations in writing. One suggested solution to the problem of non-participating pupils that I received from other researchers was to put down my pen and paper and leave these pupils out of the description. In many situations, however, this was not as easy as it first sounded. Of relevance here are arguments both that what anthropologists study is actually "the collective" rather than individuals (cf. Øye & Bjelland 2012) and that they study not individuals, but interactions and products of human interaction (Strathern 2000a). These arguments are of particular relevance to me, as I came to study pupils' notions of community and boundary drawing (Smette 2015).

It was easy for me to abstain from interviewing pupils who were not participating and to avoid being in the classroom if a majority of the pupils had not consented to participation. I found that the most difficult issue regarding the non-participating pupils had to do with the categories those pupils represented, and I faced this challenge in both schools. At Lakeside, the main problem was that some minority girls, defined by many pupils as belonging to the same collective, were not participating in the study because, according to the teachers, their parents had not consented. At Woodside, many of the non-participants were boys who were referred to as "problem kids" by teachers and some of the other pupils, part of the reason for their non-participation I explained above.

In both schools, the categories that these pupils represented were, in my experience, critically important for understanding the social dynamics among the pupils. If I left the categories they represented out of my analyses, I would not be able to represent the social dynamics of the respective schools accurately. Yet the dilemma was that if I included them in my analyses, would I be guilty of not respecting their (and their parents') decision not to participate?

My way of tackling this problem in the text was to describe and use the category labels assigned to these pupils by their peers, but to abstain from providing any information whatsoever about the individual pupils to whom the labels referred. While this way out of the dilemma may not be perfect, I regarded it as a compromise between representing the collectives accurately and respecting pupils' and parents' decisions not to participate in the research.

In the information letters that I distributed at the beginning of the school year, I promised that pupils, teachers and schools would be anonymous in the book I was going to write, and that the information I was collecting would be treated confidentially. I did not, however, specify anonymity at what level. As Walford (2008) points out, anonymity of schools in ethnographic school studies is extremely hard to achieve, particularly without leaving out so much contextual information about the school that one runs the risks of "spurious generalisability" (p. 35). Even more difficult is what we may call internal anonymity – in other words, whether people will be recognisable to others within the setting itself.

In a conversation with a data protection adviser regarding another research project that was going to take place in a school, I was told that if, say, only one person of Somali background were in a classroom, I could not describe that person as Somali, since the person would then not be anonymous. This is, of course, correct. However, in descriptions of classroom situations, it is not obvious what exact piece of information will lead to the identification of a person. Pupils' knowledge about each other is complex and includes the ability to recognise someone from the particular way an individual acts. A person is therefore likely to be recognisable from a description of his or her relationships and personal characteristics, even if what is technically identified as sensitive personal information is left out.

Anonymity is therefore very hard to achieve in ethnographic descriptions. In her ethnography of mental illness in Ireland, Scheper-Hughes experienced the difficulty of using conventional forms of anonymisation (Scheper-Hughes 1979). In hindsight, twenty-five years after the study was conducted, she offered the following reflections on how she would have proceeded differently.

> I would be inclined to avoid the "cute" and "conventional" use of pseudonyms. Nor would I attempt to scramble certain identifying features of the individuals portrayed on the naive assumption that these masks and disguises could not be rather easily de-coded by villagers themselves. I have come to see that the time-honored practice of bestowing anonymity on "our" communities and informants fools few and protects no one – save, perhaps, the anthropologist's own skin. And I fear that the practice makes rogues of us all – too free with our pens, with the government of our tongues, and with our loose translations and interpretations of village life.
>
> (Scheper-Hughes 2000: 128)

In my own study, I nonetheless decided to use pseudonyms, both for places and for people. However, I described people in ways whereby they may be recognisable to others who were present in that collective at that time. An alternative solution would have been to change certain characteristics of people to mask their identities from others. However, my conviction is that this would have led to a less truthful portrayal of the sites and the people and would likely have been less than satisfying for the people described.

With my solution to the problem of anonymity comes a critical concern: not to breach promises of confidentiality. In other words, information obtained in interviews and other confidential conversations must be linked to descriptions of a person in public settings in a very careful manner. In my analyses, therefore, I to a very limited extent drew on information I obtained in interviews when I deal with cases involving extensive descriptions of pupils in classroom situations. In the instances where I did combine such sources of information it was on the grounds that I considered the information I presented as not having the potential to inflict harm.

Also relevant here is a distinction between the kind of confidential information that is shared only by a few and "confidential" information that is shared by many. An example of the latter came up when a Lakeside teacher wanted me to confirm that I was aware of a particular girl's home situation before telling me about an interaction she had had with the girl. The girl's difficulties were well known among most of the pupils, and I interpreted the teacher's question of my familiarity with the girl's circumstances as an inquiry into whether I was already part of the community in which this information was collective knowledge. If I were, then the teacher's sharing of information with me would not be a breach of her professional ethics.

The fact that the pupil collectives described here no longer exist is relevant in terms of what may represent a risk of harm. The teachers in my two fieldwork schools and in other school studies may, in a sense, be more vulnerable than the young people; when school-based studies like mine are published, the teachers may still be working in the schools, whereas their pupils may have gone and scattered. This point ties in with Øye et al.'s (2007) critique of assumptions in formal research ethics about who counts as vulnerable groups within institutions.

Concluding remarks

After completing the study, and in the context of starting up another one, a data protection adviser told me that the rules had now become stricter regarding ethnographic research in classrooms where not all the pupils participated in research. Therefore, the general recommendation would be that the researcher provided alternative activities, in a different room, for pupils who were not part of the study. It goes without saying that with such requirements, I would not have been able to carry out my own research, and participant observation-based research in classrooms would most likely become impossible. This is a concern raised also with regard to other institutional contexts (Øye & Bjelland 2012).

In my view, it is important that the social practices taking place within central societal institutions, such as schools, can be researched, discussed and critiqued. The examples provided in this chapter illustrate possible solutions to how ethnographic research in classrooms can be carried out, also when everyone in those classrooms was not participating. A premise underlying my approach is that classrooms and school yards are semi-public settings and that the interest of an individual not to be present in a context where research takes place can be subordinated to the public interest in transparent, open schools and classrooms.

The critical question is whether the presence and the practices of the researcher have the potential of inflicting harm on those who do not wish to participate but who are still present in the field of research. The main ethical and methodological challenge in the study described here was to find a way to do ethically sound ethnographic research in what I have chosen to call partially participating collectives. Based on the discussions here, I would propose the following ways forward for ethnographic research in schools.

> First, I suggest making the process of obtaining consent an object of analysis. If researchers omit description and analysis of this process, they may miss the opportunity to reflect on how people's decision to participate, or not to participate, may be revealing of the relationships between the institutions and different categories of people.

> Second, people's initial non-consent to participation can be renegotiated, also when doing research on minors in schools. This renegotiation may take place in an ethically sound way if the researcher inspires trust and confidence in the field.

> Third, I suggest that ethnographers should be careful to make distinctions between internal and external anonymity, and between confidentiality and anonymity. Even if ethics boards and other relevant bodies may warn researchers against promising participants anonymity, the concept is difficult to escape because it is so central to most people's understanding of what protecting identities mean. A possible solution is to explain to research participants what internal and external anonymity entails and how the researcher deals with it. Linked to this, in the process of writing, the researcher must consider carefully when internal anonymity is necessary and when it is not. The litmus test should be the notion of harm, and the question: when is there a risk of inflicting harm if people who were present in a situation recognise each other, and when is there no such risk? Researchers also need to reflect on the consequences of her methods to secure both internal and external anonymity; e.g., through altering pieces of information: at what point does it compromise the trustworthiness of the analysis?

This chapter has illustrated how concerns stemming from formal and everyday ethics are interwoven in intricate ways. Ethnographers need to continue the discussion of how to conduct participant observation in institutional settings and how to represent collectives that include individuals who have not consented to participate. They must do so because formalised requirements do not provide ready answers to all the ethical and methodological dilemmas that may arise when carrying out research in practice. Instead, the examples provided here illustrate how many research ethical dilemmas are located at the intersection of everyday and formal research ethics, and that, therefore, researchers can benefit from regarding formalised and everyday ethics as connected dimensions of the research process.

Note

1 Personal data may be "directly identifiable" through name, social security number, photos or video recording, or "indirectly identifiable" through a combination of background information such as gender, work or age. The collection of *sensitive* personal data, which, according to the Norwegian Data Protection Act, include information about religious or ethnic affinity, union membership, political views and sexual orientation, tend to raise the age limit for ability to consent. If primary informants provide information about parents or guardians, information about third parties, parental or guardian consent is also required.

References

Backe-Hansen, E. 2009. "Forskning på bestemte grupper: Barn". www.etikkom.no/FBIB/Temaer/Forskning-pa-bestemte-grupper/Barn/.

Fluehr-Lobban, C. 2003a. *Ethics and the Profession of Anthropology: Dialogue for Ethically Conscious Practice*, 2nd edn. Walnut Creek, CA: AltaMira Press.

Fluehr-Lobban, C. 2003b. "Informed consent in anthropological research: We are not exempt". In *Ethics and the Profession of Anthropology: Dialogue for Ethically Conscious Practice*, edited by C. Fluehr-Lobban, XV, 278 s. Walnut Creek, CA: AltaMira Press.

Lederman, R. 2006. "The perils of working at home: IRB 'mission creep' as context and content for an ethnography of disciplinary knowledges". *American Ethnologist* 33(4): 482–491.

Mapedzahama, V. and Dune, T. 2017. "A clash of paradigms? Ethnography and ethics approval". *Sage Open* 7(1). doi: 2158244017697167.

Øye, C. and Bjelland, A.K. 2012. "Deltagende observasjon i fare? En vurdering av noen forskningsetiske retningslinjer og godkjenningsprosedyrer". *Norsk Antropologisk Tidsskrift* 23(2): 143–157.

Øye, C., Bjelland, A.K. and Skorpen, A. 2007. "Doing participant observation in a psychiatric hospital – Research ethics resumed". *Social Science & Medicine* 65(11): 2296–2306.

Pollock, K. 2012. "Procedure versus process: Ethical paradigms and the conduct of qualitative research". *BMC Medical Ethics* 13: 25.

Scheper-Hughes, N. 1979. *Saints, Scholars, and Schizophrenics: Mental Illness in Rural Ireland*. Berkeley, CA: University of California Press.

Scheper-Hughes, N. 2000. "Ire in Ireland". *Ethnography* 1(1): 117–140.

Silverman, M. 2003. "Everyday ethics: A personal journey in rural Ireland, 1980–2001". In *The Ethics of Anthropology: Debates and Dilemmas*, edited by P. Caplan, 115–132. London and New York: Routledge.

Smette, I. 2015. "The final year: An anthropological study of community in two secondary schools in Oslo, Norway". No. 505, Department of Social Anthropology, Faculty of Social Sciences, University of Oslo.

Strathern, M. 2000a. "Afterword: accountability . . . and ethnography". In *Audit Cultures: Anthropological Studies in Accountability, Ethics and the Academy*, edited by M. Strathern, 279–304. London and New York: Routledge.

Strathern, M. 2000b. *Audit Cultures: Anthropological Studies in Accountability, Ethics and the Academy, European Association of Social Anthropologists*. London: Routledge.

Walford, G. 2008. *How to Do Educational Ethnography, Ethnography and Education*. London: Tufnell press.

Chapter 5

Ethical research practice in educational institutions

Engaging with vulnerable participants

Hugh Busher

Introduction

This chapter discusses the continuing responsibilities of researchers for protecting research participants from harm throughout the life of a research project and not just at its inception to meet the ethical codes promulgated by research regulatory bodies. In particular, it focuses on how researchers can work ethically with vulnerable participants in education.

In Britain, as in many other countries in Europe and North America, researchers have a moral duty to promote "respect for the person (participants, researchers, and people in situations in which the research is carried out), knowledge, democratic values, the quality of educational research, academic freedom" (British Educational Research Association (BERA) 2018: 6). For example, in Scandinavian countries lessons on how to research ethically form an important element in research training (Beach & Eriksson 2010). Ethical codes of practice for researchers are promulgated by research bodies and research-based institutions in Europe and North America to remind researchers in what manner they should think about acting when constructing research projects. However, "many more ethical questions emerge than one could address through formal institutional reviews. Behaving ethically in the field is a complex, dynamic endeavour for education ethnographers" (Dennis 2010: 23). Ethnographic research, of its very nature, is situational and often evolves in unexpected ways with which a researcher needs to cope if ethical practice is to be sustained (Levinson 2010) especially when practices by participants or others in the field of research conflict with the values of the researcher (Barbour 2010).

The ethical codes promulgated by institutional ethical review boards seem to point to a utilitarian view of research – informed consent by participants, avoidance of harm, confidentiality of data. A researchers' duty of care for participants and their environments goes beyond just trying to prevent participants or their environment from coming to harm in the same way that caring for people means more than just keeping them safe. It also involves nurturing participants' development and wellbeing, i.e., it assumes at least a deontological (human rights) stance on ethical values and practices. This emphasises reciprocity between researchers and participants who should be treated fairly. It encourages research projects that will benefit society, not just researchers or their employers. However, Beach and Eriksson (2010) point out that even a deontological approach is flawed as it assumes a parity of social, political and economic power between people that is naive and does not reflect the realities of social interactions within the broader contexts of institutions and local and national societies. They cite the work of Flinders (1992) to indicate that relational or ecological stances to ethics in research might be more appropriate, especially for critical ethnographers, as these stances acknowledge the need to create more equal power relationships between researchers and research participants and their environments.

A researcher's duty of care is part of a moral or value-laden approach to carrying out good (effective and morally sound) research from which participants benefit by enhancing their wellbeing and personal development as well as the researcher (through gaining experiences, knowledge and publications) and a wider civic society (through gaining trustworthy knowledge outcomes from a project). Traianou (2019) in this book argues that good research requires skilful researchers to take situationally appropriate decisions that reflect particular values that lead to good practice in both moral and practical terms. In part, researchers achieve this through continually reflecting on their work in the field with the communities of which they become part as ethnographers, since they often inhabit such places for long periods of time (Dennis 2009).

Researchers' ethical practices are intended to build trust with participants and ensure trustworthy outcomes from a research project. These can only be achieved with the direct and indirect contributions of colleagues, collaborators and others according to the Economic and Social Research Council (ESRC) (2015) in Britain. To help develop ethical practice, researchers need to define what are the purposes and who are the beneficiaries of a research project as well as defining what are the relationships they wish to build with participants. The last will reflect a researcher's view of the power relationships between researchers and participants that a researcher considers acceptable. These values, intentions and related practices will need to be explained by a researcher to putative participants in and gatekeepers of a project before it can be started.

Researchers need to be particularly careful when their projects focus on sensitive topics (e.g., underage smoking, political views, sex), or involve accessing administrative records containing sensitive information about people. Such foci necessarily engender the possibility of causing harm to participants. Other projects that impinge on participant's privacy, such as those that necessarily require deception rather than first gaining participants' full and informed consent, or those inducing physical or psychological stress, such as anxiety or humiliation through collecting personal data in various ways, risk causing participants harm (ESRC 2015). The moral responsibilities of researchers deepen when their participants include people who are deemed vulnerable or are in situations that make them vulnerable.

Who are the vulnerable participants and situations?

This section attempts to indicate who might be considered vulnerable participants and what types of situation make participants vulnerable when carrying out research in education. Vulnerable people are often members of marginalised socioeconomic groups in society because of their gender, class, religion or ethnicity who sometimes inhabit marginal places and spaces, too. Vulnerable people lack power to assert themselves or to assert control over a situation especially if they are in a dependent relationship with institutional or family gatekeepers who control access to them (ESRC 2015).

Children arguably fit into this definition especially if they have disabilities, specific learning difficulties or cognitive impairment. In schools and other educational institutions, they have limited formal power because of their age and status but can assert some influence informally through negotiations and discussions with others, including staff. Students' status and actions are constrained by rules supporting social structures (Giddens 1984), which staff in educational institutions construct in order to police social interactions in an institution. These are enacted by staff persuading or coercing other people to comply with these norms that are said to be for their or other people's benefit (Lenski 1986; Foucault 1977). In educational institutions, discipline and control are inscribed on people's bodies by powerful staff requiring people to act in ways that fit with these norms if they are not to suffer socially sanctioned punishment (Foucault 1977; Paechter 2007). Although participation in formal school arenas, such as school councils, are claimed to help students' assert their agency by making their voices heard, these social structures also allow senior staff to direct the agenda of discussions and survey what is being said by whom (Fielding 2006). Further, there are doubts about which students' voices are heard through these arenas. Rainio and Hilppö (2017), through a study of early years children in Finland, debated the different forms that children's agency might take, especially when adults may be less than understanding about supporting it.

Studying marginal groups of vulnerable people in schools helps teachers and students to better understand the social processes of schools although it might involve risks to participants. Kjaran and Jóhannesson (2015) studied the construction of queer spaces in two Icelandic secondary schools and how this led to inclusion and exclusion. In this study the researchers interviewed five former and current lesbian, gay, bisexual and transgender (LGBT) students from the two schools and described how different spaces were constructed through the discourse of heterosexuality and hegemonic gender performances. Listening to young children, who can be considered vulnerable because of their age and their potential lack of understanding of a researcher's purposes and processes when these are explained to them, nonetheless allows teachers to hear students' views on their learning preferences and potentially transform their teaching practices to meet these. Students also gain a sense of agency as members of a community of learners, as Nabhani, Busher and Bahous (2012) discovered when researching with elementary school children in Lebanon. In Germany and England, Huf (2013) studied the agency of early childhood education children during their transitions to formal schooling potentially helping teachers to understand how to sustain this quality during children's transitions. However, the study raises questions about how to help the children understand and agree to the research processes proposed.

People can be made vulnerable by the topics that researchers choose to investigate, such as participants who engage in illegal or apparently anti-social activities. Högberg (2011) carried out a study in two boy-dominated classes in a vocational programme in a Swedish upper-secondary school to find out boys' perspectives on cheating during lessons and tests within academic subjects that the boys often regarded as boring or useless in relation to their future work. The boys perceived cheating as a matter of fun that expressed their anti-school attitudes, but their identities needed protecting as their views disagreed with those of staff. Green (2009) investigated students' understandings of values, discipline and school ethos in a Christian City Technology College in England. Although most students accepted the core Christian values that staff promoted as being valuable to the school and themselves, some thought the discipline that emerged from the values a little harsh at times. In both studies, the researcher needed to protect the participants from harm since the views they expressed could have been annoying to more powerful people in their schools.

People can be made vulnerable by the contexts in which researchers choose to work. Research carried out by Slobodzian (2009) investigated the experiences of deaf students in a supposedly inclusive mainstream school in the USA but found that practice tended to marginalise and exclude the deaf students. The deaf students were vulnerable because of their disability and needed to have their identities protected because their views conflicted with official cultural messages. Russell (2013) researched the experiences of marginalised young people who were not in education, employment or training in the north of England. She faced challenges in gaining and maintaining access to them, carrying out multi-site ethnography with them and recording the sociopolitical contexts to reveal how the young people experienced ethics, power and consent.

Studying marginalised social groups, such as children and young people excluded from school, also makes participants vulnerable because it shows their members to be part of a marginalised social group. Robinson and Smyth (2016) investigated excluded students in Australia and found them often to be the victims of school cultures emphasising educational performance rather than personal development. While the views of the students gave interesting insights into tensions in a school community, their identities had to be protected as staff professed differing and antagonistic views. Brüggen and Labhart (2013) investigated the emotional work of teachers in Timeout Schools in Switzerland as they tried to encourage young people who had been excluded from mainstream schools to re-engage with learning. Again, students' identities had to be protected because of the context and the differing views of powerful staff. Cross (2012) carried out research with six- and seven-year-old girls in socially disadvantaged urban communities in Scotland, despite national discourses on constructing inclusive communities, to find out what sort of communities they wanted to live in. The intrinsically vulnerable participants had to be protected from harm as their views clashed with official discourses.

People can also be made vulnerable by how researchers record the contexts of their research, which are needed to help to explain some of the views expressed by participants. For example, social artefacts within educational institutions, such as wall displays of students' work, school rules posted in classrooms, collected artefacts in cabinets in prominent public areas of a school, honour boards and photographs, tell researchers, participants and audiences of research projects a great deal about an institution's practices, its values, its rituals, its hierarchies and its processes/flows of power. Others are documents from the internal and external sociopolitical contexts of a project which exert important influences on the actions of members of educational institutions both directly through regulations about how, for example, a subject should be taught, and indirectly through the interpretations of others such as senior members of an educational institution. Researchers need to be aware that recording these social artefacts raises questions about how to protect research participants and their institutions from potential harm by making them visible, especially if school logos or names appear in some of them.

People can be made vulnerable by the types of research design a researcher chooses (ESRC 2015). If, for example, a research project distracts students from their everyday learning activities it potentially disadvantages or harms students in their studies. Using video recordings or taking photographs of classrooms or school social interactions risks making participants visible and therefore vulnerable unless the data are handled carefully (Cremin, Mason & Busher 2011). If deception is an essential part of a research design, which per se makes participants vulnerable, researchers need to make participants aware of what procedures have been used immediately after the research has finished and offer support to any participants who are distressed by their experiences of the research (BERA 2018). Webster and Marques da Silva (2013) point out that entering new worlds, such as the online sphere, poses new challenges to researchers about how to keep participants safe when researching with participants who may be living across online and offline spaces. For example, Burgess (2010) studied adult literacy students who were (re)constructing their identities as learners with their tutors using online and offline communication. Busher and James (2015) discuss the ethical dilemmas of researching on social media as their mature adult participants (re)constructed their identities as learners through online/offline interactions.

Engaging with vulnerable participants

Researchers can reduce research participants' vulnerabilities through various strategies. One of these is to reflect deeply and regularly on the ethics of their research practices through all the phases of a project, including its publication.

Another is to disabuse children and vulnerable adults of the idea that they have no choice but to take part in a research project because an authoritative person such as a teacher or school principal has asked them to do so or because a parent has agreed to them taking part. However, changes in situations and the people in them, as well as in the wider contexts of situations, mean that the examples given may not work in other times and places.

Constructing ethical practices for the field

When carrying out research with children and young people in institutions, BERA (2018) requires its members to comply with Articles 3 and 12 of the United Nations Convention on the Rights of the Child (1989). Researchers need to comply with the spirit of these articles when working with vulnerable adults, too. Children may be less able to grasp the advantages and "costs" of taking part in a research project because they lack either the language or the conceptual understanding to make sense of what researchers might tell them about a project before they join it. Consequently, researchers need to tailor carefully their explanations of a research project and what participating in it might involve to meet the language and conceptual capacities of the children or vulnerable adults, e.g., second-language learners, or people with learning difficulties with whom they are going to work (Knobel 2005).

Ethical practice begins before researchers enter the field by researchers working out how to develop trusting relationships with their participants, especially if the children are young or said to be challenging (Barley & Bath 2014; Gillies & Robinson 2010). The process includes "becoming acquainted with the norms and beliefs of the field location, learning how to locate and build relationships, unobtrusively collecting and recording data, and 'mapping the setting'" (Barley & Bath 2014: 192) but these topics also need to be addressed reflexively throughout the life of a research project. Building closer relationships with participants before the start of a project helps to build trust and improve the quality of the data gathered, as Dicks (2013), in a study of primary school children in Wales using science discovery centres, also noted. However, Lefstein (2010), through a study of a failing primary school in London, explored the dangers of researchers becoming too close to their participants and making visible their own views on topics relevant to the research.

Building closer relationships with participants helps to develop trust with them. This is closely related to a belief by research project participants that they are respected and have a sense of ownership of and influence on the processes of the project. To begin to construct trust, researchers need to make clear to potential participants, in a language that participants can understand, what are the purposes of the project, how participants and other people might benefit from the research (Robson & Robson 2002), what part potential participants are being asked to play in the project and what will be the "costs" of their participation. The "costs" will include the amount of time and types of activity that joining a project is likely to generate. The benefits might include experiencing being in a research project, experiencing certain research techniques, receiving a summary of the final research report and, altruistically, contributing to knowledge that will make a difference to society. Further, researchers need to explain to potential participants what social and interpersonal values are enshrined in a project, what are the potential ethical risks in the study (Sikes 2006) and how the researchers intend to manage these issues (James & Busher 2006). However, the construction of trust may not always be as easy to implement as researchers might hope, especially when trying to develop participatory research with challenging students (Gillies & Robinson 2010).

The purposes and processes of a research project can be clarified to potential participants by constructing a rubric for a project and its data collection processes (James & Busher 2009). Participants can be engaged in helping to develop the codification of these, although this can be problematic if students are doubtful about taking part (Gillies & Robinson 2010). Part of the management of data collection might include giving participants the opportunity to "opt out" during a project, e.g., their right to refuse to participate in certain processes. For example, they might choose not to be observed as part of a lesson or not to have certain things they say recorded during an interview. Researchers need to agree with participants when to stop a digital recorder being used for interviews. . . and when to start it again. Another part will include storing data in a secure manner to protect participants from accidental harm. This is especially important with interview transcripts, observation records (including photographs), online discussions or institutional documents where participants' names or other identifiers may be embedded in the research records. All information, especially textual or visual information stored electronically, must be rendered anonymous when storing it, as it can be migrated very easily outside the research project community. Personal information about participants and their institutions should not normally be stored mechanically or electronically with research information from them to avoid contagion from juxtaposed records. Nor should any irrelevant data to the specific purposes of a research project be collected and stored (ESRC 2015). Researchers using online sites need to ensure that electronic data curation (storage) is sufficiently safe for the purposes of their research project (James & Busher 2009).

Researchers also need to make clear how the dissemination of a project's outcomes will continue to protect participants from harm. Data collected for a study should only be used in ways that are compatible, "with the original purpose of the project" (Elgesem 2002: 201). For example, it is unethical to use extracts from project data for teaching purposes, especially if not properly anonymised, or to share it with other people, if participants have not given their express permission for that. This is because people's conversations in written or electronic form or their visual social artefacts are their social products, not those of the researchers.

Only after participants are clear about the ways in which researchers intend to carry out a project and keep participants and their institutions safe from harm should researchers ask them to give their informed consent to participate in a project by giving them consent forms to complete. Giving informed consent acknowledges people's fundamental democratic rights to freedom and self-determination, including choosing to join on not to join a project free from coercion or bribery (ESRC 2015) and having the right to withdraw at any time from it. However, some people in some cultures are unwilling to give written consent and researchers need to find means of coping with that, such as keeping a list of participants with a note to say who has consented verbally, with the permission of the participants. Swain (2018) offers an interesting, if problematic, insight in to this by discussing how to record and use informal conversations in the research field, questioning also where that field might be deemed to end. To help vulnerable participants understand more clearly what they are doing when they are giving informed consent in a project that is likely to develop through time, as many ethnographic studies do, Renold and Edwards (2018), in two different projects with vulnerable participants in Wales, created collections of objects to explore with the putative participants what was meant by anonymity, harm and confidentiality, especially when working with visual and online data. Further, as an ethnographic study progresses researchers may need to involve new people in it, so they then need to gain the informed consent of the new participants to participate.

Demonstrating ethical research practice in the field

Researchers have to walk the talk, as well as talk the talk, about ethical practice with participants, and even then it can be difficult for researchers to help participants to engage willingly with a project (Gillies & Robinson 2010). One of the ways of enacting ethical research practice is for researchers to be aware of the spaces they and their participants are using, including online spaces, when collecting data through talking with or observing participants. In some contexts, researchers need to be careful about the spaces they use with participants if of the opposite sex to the participants, especially if the researchers are male (Shah 2004). In educational institutions, researchers need to reflect carefully on what constitutes a private or a public space and how easy it is to communicate with participants in a given space because of, for example, background noise, or who else may be listening to or overhearing a research conversation. They also need to be aware of whom they are listening/talking to or of whom they are observing and their social position – for example, whether or not they occupy a post of formal responsibility – since their status may affect the views or actions they express.

Knowing what data should or should not be recorded during interviews and observations is also an aspect of ethical practice. Researchers may have to decide whether it is proper or appropriate even to record certain information offered by participants, such as information that is detrimental to participants or their institutions, or unsupported opinions about other participants or institutions whether or not part of the study. It also requires researchers to ensure that research conversations and other information are recorded and stored (curated) securely and not used as a source of general tittle-tattle inside or outside a research project.

Researchers need to be respectful about how participants prefer to record information and what information to record to take account of participants' cultural contexts. In some contexts, researchers of the opposite sex to the participants or of a different ethnic group or cultural community may make some participants feel uncomfortable and unwilling to share their views openly in interviews, or to be observed (Shah 2004). In other contexts there is suspicion about how electronic recordings might be used or there are taboos about who or what may be photographed or video recorded (James & Busher 2009). Clearly demarcated social and power differentials between researchers and participants, such as that between children and adults, or between adults of different formal status in a school or college, has a similar impact.

Researchers also need to indicate clearly to research project participants, gatekeepers of research sites and people not connected with a research project what they can, ethically, discuss about a project. For example, it is unethical for researchers to pass judgement on any practices seen on a research site or any views expressed by research participants or other members of the research site, even if people ask a researcher for such a comment. The same vow of silence needs to be sustained outside the research site when talking with other people, even if they are research-oriented colleagues, as commenting on events or persons on a research site breaches the confidentiality that researchers offer to their participants to keep them safe from harm and ensure that their privacy and dignity is not impaired. Further, such tittle-tattle might make visible the sites of a project, even if unintentionally.

Building inclusive research practices

Research project cultures are social constructs (Giddens 1984) based on participants' values, interests and lived experiences in various communities, and their cultural and social capital. Although people's social relationships are tied to the social frameworks from which they come (Giddens 1991), researchers can respect participants' cultural plurality by structuring research projects to take account of participants cultural preferences. Constructing collaborative and value-laden practices by researchers are intended not only to sustain the engagement of participants in a project but also to sustain the professional integrity of a project's design, the generation and analysis of data, and the publication of results (ESRC 2015). The language used in research projects between researchers and participants, too, can help to construct cultures of engagement that might help participants to engage more cheerfully with a project (Knobel 2005), although this might be hard to construct with challenging students (Gillies & Robinson 2010).

Every participant in a research project learns, as well as helping to construct knowledge to achieve a research project's intended purposes. Constructing supportive cultures in research projects helps researchers to facilitate participants' learning about research processes and indicates respectfulness for them. For example, a researcher can take care to meet participants for research conversations at times convenient to the participant or to meet them online asynchronously. Further, supportive cultures help vulnerable participants to benefit from involvement in research by developing their identities and voices through having their views on situations valued. Children and young people, marginalised subordinates in educational processes, can offer important insights as expert witnesses of teaching, learning and educational institutional practices, in part through their long experiences of those practices. In turn, this raises participants' self-esteem and sense of agency by recognising their importance as people and as participants in school/college processes.

Taking part in other people's research projects helps vulnerable people to gain insights into how to carry out research and analyse research data, especially if they are actively involved in helping to gather data in somebody else's project, as well as being sources of data in it themselves (Busher, Lewis & Comber 2014). Participation helps young people to be able to "speak out" about matters that concern them; to prepare themselves to be citizens in a democratic society; and helps policymakers and school staff to understand and respect the world of young people (Flutter & Ruddock 2004: 101). Being participant researchers allows vulnerable people to reflect on their own practice and clarify their views of it in relation to an educational institution's processes and policy contexts, as a study by Milstein (2010) with primary school children in Argentina showed. Participation also helps to improve the quality of the data collected, as it did in a study by Dicks (2013).

Participatory research can take many forms, such as developing participatory videos (Patience 2007) or constructing story boards or visual tours (Pink 2009) or through making scrapbooks of participants' experiences in educational situations (Cremin, Mason & Busher 2011). Constructing these artefacts helps students to develop a sense of agency and allows them to control the agenda of their presentations by first choosing what photographs they want to take or scenes they want to shoot and then arranging them into meaningful sequences to communicate their ideas to audiences, such as student colleagues, teachers, parents and academic researchers. They also help students to understand through practice the ethics of carrying out research by helping student researchers to recognise the rights of others to respect and anonymity if they desire it and the practices needed to carryout visual ethnography ethically. These artefacts also leave students with a tangible record of the research study if they are defined as the property of the student participants which they can keep after the end of the project.

Conclusion

This chapter has discussed how researchers can enact research ethically with participants in educational institutions, especially those who might be deemed vulnerable. What factors can contribute to participants being deemed vulnerable has been extensively discussed, as well as how researchers might be able to help vulnerable participants to develop their identities as people able to assert their agency through taking part in research projects. This discussion has been predicated on understanding researchers' duty of care for research participants as going beyond what is often required in various institutional ethical codes of keeping participants safe from harm. It has also been predicated on researchers continuing reflexively throughout the life of a research project to consider how to implement ethical practice in the field and not to rely on the requirements of what institutional ethical review boards deem as appropriate ethical procedures merely at the start of a project.

References

Barbour, A. 2010. "Exploring some ethical dilemmas and obligations of the ethnographer". *Ethnography and Education* 5(2): 159–173.

Barley, R. and Bath, C. 2014. "The importance of familiarisation when doing research with young children". *Ethnography and Education* 9(2): 182–195.

Beach, D. and Eriksson, A. 2010. "The relationship between ethical positions and methodological approaches: a Scandinavian perspective". *Ethnography and Education* 5(2): 129–142.

British Educational Research Association (BERA). 2018. *Ethical Guidelines for Educational Research*, 4th edn. London. www.bera.ac.uk/researchers-resources/publications/ethical-guidelines-for-educational-research-2018.

Brüggen, S. and Labhart, C.K. 2013. "Emotion work in timeout schools". *Ethnography and Education* 8(3): 338–354.

Burgess, A. 2010. "The use of space-time to construct identity and context". *Ethnography and Education* 5(10): 17–31.

Busher, H. and James, N. 2015. "In pursuit of ethical research: studying hybrid communities using online and face-to-face communications". *Educational Research and Evaluation: An International Journal on Theory and Practice, Special Issue on Ethical Issues in Online Research* 21(2): 168–181.

Busher, H., Lewis, G. and Comber, C. 2014. "Living and learning as an international postgraduate student at a Midlands university". *Journal of Further and Higher Education* 40(1): 48–64.

Cremin, H., Mason, C. and Busher, H. 2011. "Problematising pupil voice using visual methods: findings from a study of engaged and disaffected pupils in an urban secondary school". *British Educational Research Journal* 37(4): 585–603.

Cross, B. 2012. "How does community matter? Misrecognition and the participation agenda for children in socially disadvantaged communities". *Ethnography and Education* 7(3): 311–326.

Dennis, B. 2009. "What does it mean when an ethnographer intervenes?" *Ethnography and Education* 4(2): 131–146.

Dennis, B. 2010. "Ethical dilemmas in the field: the complex nature of doing education ethnography". *Ethnography and Education* 5(2): 123–127.

Dicks, B. 2013. "Interacting with . . . what? Exploring children's social and sensory practices in a science discovery centre". *Ethnography and Education* 8(3): 301–322.

Economic and Social Research Council (ESRC). 2015. *Framework for Research Ethics.*

Elgesem, D. 2002. "What is special about the ethical issues in online research?" *Ethics and Information Technology* 4: 195–203.

Fielding, M. 2006. "Leadership, radical collegiality and the necessity of person-centred education". *International Journal of Leadership in Education* 9(4): 299–313.

Flutter, J. and Ruddock, J. 2004. *How to Improve Your School: Giving Pupils a Voice.* London: Continuum Books.

Foucault, M. 1977. *Discipline and Punish: The Birth of the Prison*, trans. A. Sheridan. London: Allen Lane.

Giddens, A. 1984. *The Constitution of Society.* Berkley, CA: University of California.

Giddens, A. 1991. *Modernity and Self-Identity.* Cambridge: Polity Press.

Gillies, V. and Robinson, Y. 2010. "Managing emotions in research with challenging pupils". *Ethnography and Education* 5(1): 97–110.

Green, E. 2009. "Discipline and school ethos: exploring students' reflections upon values, rules and the Bible in a Christian city technology college". *Ethnography and Education* 4(2): 197–209.

Högberg, R. 2011. "Cheating as subversive and strategic resistance: vocational students' resistance and conformity towards academic subjects in a Swedish upper secondary school". *Ethnography and Education* 6(3): 341–355.

Huf, C. 2013. "Children's agency during transition to formal schooling". *Ethnography and Education* 8(1): 61–76.

James, N. and Busher, H. 2006. "Credibility, authenticity and voice: dilemmas in online interviewing". *Qualitative Research* 6(3): 403–420.

James, N. and Busher, H. 2009. *Online Interviewing.* London: Sage.

Kjaran, J.I. and Jóhannesson, I.Á. 2015. "Inclusion, exclusion and the queering of spaces in two Icelandic upper secondary schools". *Ethnography and Education* 10(1): 42–59.

Knobel, M. 2005. "'Rants, ratings and representation: ethical issues in researching online social practices". In *Ethics and Research in Inclusive Education: Values into Practice*, edited by K. Sheehy, M. Nind, J. Rix and K. Simmons, chapter 12. London: Routledge/Falmer Open University.

Lefstein, A. 2010. "Problematising researcher–respondent relations through an exploration of communicative stance". *Ethnography and Education* 5(1): 81–96.

Lenski, G. 1986. "Power and privilege". In *Power*, edited by S. Lukes, 243–252. Oxford: Blackwell.

Levinson, M.P. 2010. "Accountability to research participants: unresolved dilemmas and unravelling ethics". *Ethnography and Education* 5(2): 193–207.

Milstein, D. 2010. "Children as co-researchers in anthropological narratives in education". *Ethnography and Education* 5(1): 1–15.

Nabhani, M., Busher, H. and Bahous, R. 2012. "Cultures of engagement in challenging circumstances: four Lebanese primary schools in urban Beirut". *School Leadership and Management* 32(1): 37–55.

Paechter, C. 2007. *Being Boys, Being Girls: Learning Masculinities and Femininities.* Abingdon: McGraw Hill.

Patience, S. 2007. *Participatory Video for Pupil Voice: An Experiment in Emancipatory Research.* M.A. dissertation, University of East Anglia.

Pink, S. 2009. "Applied and participatory methods in visual ethnography". *Introduction to Visual Methods workshop, ESRC Research Development Initiative, Building Capacity in Visual Methods.* University of Leicester, 13–14 January 2009.

Rainio, A.P. and Hilppö, J. 2017. "The dialectics of agency in educational ethnography". *Ethnography and Education* 12(1): 78–94.

Renold, E. and Edwards, V. 2018. "Making 'informed consent' matter: crafting ethical objects in participatory research with children". *Research Intelligence* 136: 22–23.

Robinson, J. and Smyth, J. 2016. "'Sent out' and *Stepping Back In*: stories from young people 'placed at risk'". *Ethnography and Education* 11(2): 222–236.

Robson, K. and Robson, M. 2002. "Your place or mine? Ethics, the researcher and the Internet". In *Ethical Dilemmas in Qualitative Research*, edited by T. Welland and L. Pigsley, 94–107. London: Ashgate.

Russell, L. 2013. "Researching marginalised young people". *Ethnography and Education* 8(1): 46–60.

Shah, S. 2004. "The researcher/interviewer in intercultural context: a social intruder!" *British Educational Research Journal* 30(4): 549–575.

Sikes, P. 2006. "On dodgy ground? Problematics and ethics in educational research". *International Journal of Research and Method in Education* 29(1): 105–117.

Slobodzian, J.T. 2009. "The devil is in the details: issues of exclusion in an inclusive educational environment". *Ethnography and Education* 4(2): 181–195.

Swain, J. 2018. "The role of informal conversations during fieldwork: where do the ethical boundaries lie?" *Research Intelligence* 136: 12–13.

Traianou, A. 2019. "*Phrónēsis* and the ethical regulation of ethnographic research". In *Implementing Ethics in Educational Ethnography: Regulation and Practice*, edited by H. Busher and A. Fox, 19–31. London: Routledge.

United Nations. 1989. *Convention on the Rights of the Child*. New York: United Nations. www.unicef.org.uk/UNICEFs-Work/UN-Convention/.

Webster, J.P. and Marques da Silva, S. 2013. "Doing educational ethnography in an online world: methodological challenges, choices and innovations". *Ethnography and Education* 8(2): 123–130.

Part III

Ethical dilemmas in the field

Chapter 6

Double agent?

Ethical considerations in conducting ethnography as a teacher-researcher

Hanna M. Nikkanen

Introduction

While developing a position of a teacher-researcher, I have aimed at making educational practice and research meet more quickly and more effectively. Working 80 per cent as a music teacher in a Finnish comprehensive school, and 20 per cent as a researcher in the University of the Arts Helsinki, I am able to bring research-based information to school practice as well as to raise current topics and to collect material from school life for research.

The key benefits of the double role are living in the field for years, possessing tacit knowledge of the teaching profession, and following the societal and educational changes in the school in real time. However, there are also ethical challenges due to the double position. How to record the daily life of the school, balancing your research interests, teaching schedule and ethical questions concerning the students? How to combine the positions as an observing researcher and as an equal and active member of the school staff? How to honor students' and teachers' right to refuse participating in my research, when I am researching the daily life of our school?

In this setting, I understand "integrity" as defined by Bruce Macfarlane (2009: 44–45), namely in addition to the research process concerning also the researcher, "integrating different parts of one's true self, physically, mentally and perhaps socially" and "linking values and identity as a person with practice as a researcher". The roles of a teacher and a researcher need not to be separated and must not be ignored, but reflected as facets of one's identity, affecting also the moral and ethical choices. Marilys Guillemin and Lynn Gillam (2004: 274) write:

> Our research interests and the research questions we pose, as well as the questions we discard, reveal something about who we are. Our choice of research design, the research methodology, and the theoretical framework that informs our research are governed by our values and reciprocally, help to shape these values.

This chapter will focus on the positionality of a teacher-researcher as a moral agent (Macfarlane 2009) when conducting ethnography. As Guillemin and Gillam above, I find the double role of a teacher-researcher informing all the phases of the research. Therefore, reflection is also needed, not only as the final phase of the research project, but throughout the process. I will discuss ethical considerations concerning both the students and the colleagues, moments of reflection and my solutions on how to define the topics and design the methods when conducting ethnography in my own educational community.

Ethical principles of teachers and researchers

In Finland, the professional ethical codes of teachers and educational ethnographers are mainly overlapping. Both professions are regulated by laws and other norms, for example, curricula or ethical principles of research given by national or international boards. Yet, in both professions, knowing legislation and regulation is necessary but still only a starting point for ethical action. In addition, both professions have their ethical norms and morals. While both teachers and ethnographers work in the field, interacting with people in their daily life, the work can neither be totally planned and controlled beforehand, nor regulated in every detail. Often unforeseen situations require quick decisions on how to react and quick evaluation on whether the planned activity is still relevant.

In Finland, ethical principles of research have been published separately for the humanities and social and behavioural sciences (TENK 2009), and the ethical approval process considering qualitative, non-medical research is relatively smooth. As for school ethnographies, ethical review process is not necessarily needed at all, if "the head teacher of a school has evaluated that the study would produce useful information for the institution or school and can be carried out as part of the normal activities of the institution or school" and if directly identifying information is not collected (TENK 2009: 6–7; TENK 2018). Even if the review process is not required, the National Advisory Board on Research Ethics (TENK) guides to pay careful attention to respectful action towards the participants through all the stages of the research by, for example, "treating subjects with respect' during the research process and 'reporting findings in a respectful way in research publications" (TENK 2009: 8).

On the other hand, universities or funding agencies may require ethical review, as is the case in the ArtsEqual project under which I currently work. The review process guides the researcher to consider the possible risks throughout the project, which acts as a precautionary process. The obvious ethical risks are eliminated, of course, but beyond that, the ethical boards work more as advisory boards, giving recommendations on what issues to consider more carefully during the research process. However, a big responsibility for the final ethical solutions is left for the researcher. The Finnish National Advisory Board on Research Ethics (TENK 2009: 13) reminds:

Evaluation never shifts responsibility for research ethics to the committee. In research in the humanities and social and behavioural sciences, ethical questions focus on the encounter between the researcher and the subject, which can include unanticipated factors. The researcher is always responsible for the ethical and moral solutions in a study.

Like researchers, teachers also work very independently in Finland. There is no school inspector system, for as the school teacher qualification requires a master's degree, teachers are expected to be able to independently plan, evaluate and develop their pedagogy, considering also ethical aspects. The Trade Union of Education in Finland (OAJ) guides teachers in their *Ethical Principles for the Teaching Profession* (OAJ 2018):

> Any consideration of the ethics of the teaching profession calls for a distinction to be made between legal and ethical matters. The basic duties and responsibilities of teachers are defined in the relevant legislation and norms, while the content of the teaching is laid down in the curriculum. By contrast, however, the ethics of the profession are not based on compulsion or external supervision but on an internalized concept of the moral obligations attached to the work.

Concurrently, the Research Council of the neighbouring country Sweden guides researchers in the *Good Research Practice* (Swedish Research Council 2017: 17) as follows.

> [O]ne must constantly distinguish between the law and morals and, when it comes to research, also between research ethics legislation and the rules found in research ethics codes. The ethical criteria can be more far-reaching than the legal requirements when their content is otherwise closely related. The ethical criteria can also address issues that do not appear in legislation at all . . . The researcher's own reflections on his or her project must instead be based on both knowledge of the content of laws and codes, and on his or her own moral judgement.

The duality of fulfilling the legal duties, on one hand, and the ethical codes on the other, has been a topic of vivid discussion during the first decades of the twenty-first century, and has also been described as "external and internal research ethics" (Swedish Research Council 2017: 12), or as "up-front and embedded ethics" (MacDonald 2017: 32). Guillemin and Gillam (2004: 263, 273) use concepts of "procedural ethics", concerning the process of designing the research taking into account the ethical issues that can be anticipated in the process and presented to the ethical review board, and "ethics in practice" concerning "the everyday ethical issues that arise in the doing of research". The Swedish Research Council makes a distinction between research ethics and professional ethics, the former referring to conducting the research project and the latter to "the researcher's responsibility towards research and research community" (Swedish Research Council 2017: 12). As professional ethics is here understood as containing relationships to one's professional communities, in case of a teacher-researcher I read this to cover collegial communities both in academia and in school, as well as responsibility towards both the professions. In addition to the research community, the professional ethics would thus cover relationships to colleagues in school, the students, the communal authorities running the school, as well as teachers as a professional community. This kind of understanding of professional ethics finds resonance in Stutchbury's and Fox's (2009) concept of "relational thinking" as one of four dimensions of an ethical appraisal framework.

Despite various concepts, there seems to be consensus that the ethical matters of research are not solved once the review board has accepted the research plan. Especially ethnographers, dealing with values, beliefs and hierarchies of social communities, are likely to face the biggest challenges while in the field. They may sense "ethical tensions" (Costley & Gibbs 2006: 92) when they face "judgements that need to be made" (Stutchbury & Fox 2009: 494) or "resolve conflicts" (Hammersley 2013: 7) which may be "role conflicts" (Fox & Mitchell, Chapter 8, this volume), "moral dilemmas" (Levinson 2010) or "dilemmas of practice" (Josselsson 2007; Nichols 2016), or, when no stark choice between very different options is needed, merely "ethically important moments" (Guillemin & Gillam 2004).

Being a teacher-researcher, in moments of ethical tensions I find teacher ethics define my solutions even more than researcher ethics. Referring to my reading of professional ethics in the case of a teacher-researcher above, it is due to the great amount of relationality in a teacher's work. As a teacher, I am related to school students with more ties than I would be as a mere researcher; I am not only interested in their lives and opinions but also responsible for supervising the students in their studies in general, in group dynamics and in "good life". When a researcher as an outsider may choose to affect the daily life of the school as little as possible, as an insider I am expected to make a difference in school life. Thus, my power position is also different to that of an outsider. When conducting a research project in my school, it is not only about the integrity of the research project but also about my daily actions and relationality as a teacher, as a supervisor of the teenaged students, as a colleague, as an employee, as member of staff and as member of the sub teams. Similarly, Costley and Gibbs (2006: 91) argue that the practitioner researchers should prioritise their allegiance to their workplaces, for the aim of the research is usually developing the practice of this community, and let the academy be only the second community. Also, Fox (with Mitchell, Chapter 8, this volume) chose putting participants and local values first. Even with a permission from the ethical board to conduct my study, putting the local school values first and considering my relationality as a teacher towards my students or my colleagues, I have several times redirected my research plans. I will reflect these "ethically important moments" (Guillemin & Gillam 2004: 262) as cases in this chapter.

As a frame, I use Macfarlane's (2009: 41–42) conception of research as a series of phases, which are framing, negotiating, generating, creating and disseminating; however, when Macfarlane considers reflecting as the final phase, I will discuss reflection taking place during all the other phases and thus consider reflexivity as an "ethical notion" (Guillemin & Gillam 2004: 262).

Anonymity impossible – questions of framing

Instead of having individual key informants to get insight into the culture, I have chosen mainly to use collective group approaches.

It is necessary to design the research setting so that the research project will not harm individual participants nor the community (Swedish Research Council 2017: 13). The double role of a teacher-researcher sets special requirements in this sense. As a member of the school staff, you get to know issues and get access to places and classified files that would not be revealed to an outsider (e.g., access to staff meetings). In turn, as a member of the community, you may not get to know issues that would be told to a researcher from outside of the school. This affects both selecting the topic and the approach.

When researching one's own practice or community, it is impossible to promise full anonymity for the participants. Even when using pseudonyms for the community and the people observed, it is easy to find out the researcher's affiliation (TENK 2009: 13). Moreover, in educational ethnography, it is usually necessary to describe the age of the participants and the size of the target group, as well as the year when the research material was collected. With these identifiers, it might be possible to recognise the participants. On one hand, very intimate issues might be better left to researchers who are not connected to participants with other ties than the research. On the other hand, a carefully and respectfully designed setting and approach may allow dealing also with delicate topics in ways that would not be possible for researchers from outside of the school community.

My doctoral research (Nikkanen 2014) dealt with how musical performances may construct the educational culture and the "local moral order" (van Langenhove & Harré 1999) of a school. I worked at a school developing methods for collaborative working, supporting students with special educational needs and nurturing a sense of community. School celebrations, including various performances by student groups, were found as important elements towards these goals. The teachers found that school celebrations were not only for fun or recreation. They served the sense of community but also, as one teacher articulated, while the whole class was working for a common performance, the students "learn something that would not be learned during the normal classroom lessons" (Nikkanen 2010: 52).

I was interested in the process of preparing for a musical performance both from the viewpoint of the educational culture and of an individual student with special educational needs. It would have been interesting to follow the process of a musical performance through the eyes of one or two students. However, this would have brought up very personal information. Bearing in mind that both the teachers and students could be recognisable by some readers, I chose to approach the issue through the community lens. I conducted group interviews instead of individual interviews or diaries, and observed a whole class instead of individual students (Nikkanen 2010, 2014).

The entire pedagogical staff of the school discussed the history, the pedagogical significance and the future challenges of the practice of multiple annual celebrations in this particular school. While discussing, they negotiated a shared understanding of the educational culture of the school. Thus, they created a "collective narrative" that they could stand for as a staff.

I then observed one process of producing a musical performance by a group of second-grade (roughly eight-year-old) students and their class teacher. Instead of observing how the process looks like to one particular student with special educational needs, I chose to observe how the values and principles articulated by the staff, strongly emphasising the significance of performance processes in supporting the growth of students with special educational needs, take place in action. The teacher wanted to base the process of preparing for the performance on values of participatory agency, collaboration and fair play. The musical process demanded the students to develop their skills to cooperate in engaging these values and took place in an embodied, sometimes also very noisy way. Some of the students protested strongly when the collective decision was different from their opinion. However, observing this helped to illuminate the question: how is moral order negotiated in moments of disagreement? The chosen perspective – to observe the process of the class community instead of one child – made it easier to write about awkward moments. It allowed me to distance writing from individuals if needed. Additionally, because it was now more about group dynamics than about individual students, it allowed me to give several pseudonyms to one student when describing sensitive moments, in order to avoid several identifiers leading to recognising any student.

It is hard to hide – negotiating participation

Participation in research needs to be voluntary and one should be able at any time to quit participation in the research. However, it is hard to hide while someone is conducting ethnography in your community.

On one hand, community perspective may cover individuals, letting one simply be part of the issue observed and not the key informant. On the other hand, it may also limit one's possibilities to refuse participation in the research as an individual – especially so with children. The Finnish National Advisory

Board on Research Ethics allows observing teaching even without a consent from parents, if the project is being carried out as part of the normal school work (TENK 2009: 6). Even when families are informed of the research, the decisions about participation are often made by adults. Therefore, what is the child's possibility to refuse participation, if the everyday life of the class is agreed by teachers and parents to be observed? Is it possible for the parents to deny participation without fearing that this would affect the relationship between the child and the teacher, or even the assessment?

Also, amongst the staff, agreeing participation as a community may in effect force an individual to participate non-voluntarily. In schools, the decision about participation in a research study is usually made by a steering group or solely by the principal. Still, the individual employees can not be forced to participate (Gray 2014: 90). Yet, even though no actual coercion would take place, it may be almost impossible to refuse to participate in research if the researcher has got permission to attend your meetings or observe the daily life of your workplace. It may also be difficult to refuse if doing so would make an individual feel that they seem resistant as a colleague, as a friend or as a member of staff.

> A researcher must make sure that the principle of voluntary participation is also observed in situations where there is interaction with subjects. A subject's annoyance, embarrassment, fearfulness or physical fatigue can be sufficient grounds for the researcher to discontinue the study as far as the subject is concerned, even if the subject does not expressly refuse to continue. It is essential to ensure that subjects are participating voluntarily when studying people in institutional settings.
>
> (TENK 2009: 9; 2018)

As for students, I have asked for oral assent in addition to signed consent from parents. If a student has not wanted to be filmed or interviewed, I have honored his or her decision. Sometimes I have recorded merely the feet of the children if this was accepted, or set the camera so that the particular child is not visible. In some occasions, I have just shut the camera. As for adults, one occasion left me hesitating and led even to a change of research topic – although I eventually returned to it – as is described in the next narrative.

Narrowing the field – questions of generating data

In ethnography, it is usual to collect any possible data that may shed light on the phenomenon inquired. However, I chose to narrow the field and define the time and the venues where I collect data.

In 2014, a renewed version of the *National Core Curriculum for Basic Education* was published.[1] Compared to the previous Core Curricula, greater emphasis is laid on, e.g., crossing the borders of subjects and classrooms, active participation, the significance of the emotions and the joy of learning. The schools are expected to annually offer every student at least one multidisciplinary learning unit, that is, a unit combining contents and methods of two or more subjects.

While during the pre-school and primary school years, usually taught by class teachers, multidisciplinary approaches are widely used, I was interested in how this principle could be brought into practice in the very subject divided and forty-five-minute lesson divided tradition of the lower-secondary school. Also, I was keen to know whether it would be possible to use art-based approaches and appreciate artistic modes of learning, knowing, doing and being also when studying contents of academic subjects.

One of my research themes I named as "Arts, Academics, and Wellbeing", including the question of "How to organize collaborative planning, working, teaching and learning in teachers' and students' schedules?" I expected that the modules would be carried out within the traditional schedule, to be term- or year-long and between two or three subjects, and I started planning a module with a history teacher. On the contrary, the steering group of the school set a special team to plan the realisation of these modules. The team has innovated several possible designs, each tested within a couple of years. For example, the first module was designed in groups of six to seven teachers of various subjects and age levels. Every group was to plan one lesson on the theme space, which was then taught to every class (from first to ninth grade) within one week. I had been prepared to document the process of me and the history teachers planning how to synchronise the contents and perspectives of the music and history courses during the eighth grade. Suddenly, the planning and implementing was spread through the whole school. I tried to follow documenting, how we would overcome the challenge as teachers in an 850-student school, catering for general education, special education, music-specialised education and education for recently immigrated children. I planned to write diary notes of how the process progressed, what issues were discussed as benefits and problems, how the problems were solved and how the task was encountered emotionally. One day, I was working by the computer in the teachers' lounge while I heard some teachers discussing the process. I started writing notes, not mentioning the names of discussants, but documenting comments and interpreting emotions connected. I needed to leave the computer for a while and when I returned, a colleague, looking for a free computer to work with, made clear that she had seen my notes by asking: you are working by this computer, aren't you? Suddenly I felt guilty. I knew I had done nothing illegal; the school had accepted the role of partner school for the research project, and the teachers knew this and the subject of my research. Still, I felt like a spy disguised.

For a researcher from outside of the school, there would not have been any problem in documenting the discussion. It would also have been evident for the teachers that the researcher, when present, might be taking notes. I realised that in spite of the consents and the nature of ethnography, I should not record every aspect of the everyday life. The participants need to know when I do the research and when I am present merely in the role of a colleague or teacher.

Turning it around, I also do not want that, in my presence, colleagues would suspect that anything they say could and would be used for purposes they could not control.

I decided to terminate this research topic for I felt that it was ethically impossible to observe something so scattered in time and all over the school. Luckily, my second topic – how the school could increase accessibility of after school musical activities – turned out to be fruitful and possible to study. I continued developing the multidisciplinary and art-based practices as a teacher, and helping other researchers with their interventions in my school.

One of the interventions initialised by another researcher was a language-sensitive dance workshop for recently immigrated students. After one term of working with these small groups I suggested that we would develop the design by collaborating with a peer group of a general education class. To be able to run a larger project, we could use the week reserved for multidisciplinary learning units and connect with the common theme, Finnish nature and animals. We chose the peer group to be an eighth-grade group and, consulting the biology teacher, decided to concentrate on Finnish forests, that being a key issue in the eighth-grade biology course.

Suddenly I noticed that we had planned a multidisciplinary learning unit, using an art-based approach on an academic topic, engaging a limited number of participants, time and space. Thus, we had framed a bounded context which enabled us to document the phase as originally intended.

Teaching and researching – questions of creating results and interpretations

In participatory ethnography, the researcher should not impose personal bias in the data. However, as a teacher, I design my lessons and courses, and as a member of the staff I am expected to participate in decisions on the educational culture of the school.

My ideal in developing the position of a teacher-researcher has been bringing research-based information to school practice and bringing practice-based information from school to research. However, Macfarlane (2009: 59), for example, is doubtful about the quality of research where the researcher is part of the phenomenon, and names school teachers particularly as an example. He sees bias and ability to change the process as clear risks. Indeed, ethical honesty is required when deciding which practices are to be developed and researched, and how to act within these practices both as a teacher and as a researcher. Important questions for me to reflect upon have been: does research influence my actions as a teacher? Do I ask students to do something just because of my research? Do I favour some students or activities only to get good results as a researcher?

One solution connected to this aspect is balancing with power positions. Although being deeply interested in developing the school, I have not volunteered to be a member of the school steering group. I find it important that the steering group accepts the plans for the research interventions. I need to be able to rationalise the suggested interventions in terms of the curriculum and the good life in school to the steering group. It is also easier for my colleagues to make critical questions on my plan when they are acting as members of the steering group, being in this role above me in organisational hierarchy and speaking with the collective "mouth" of the group, than it would be in their role as my peers.

While planning the implementation of the multi-disciplinary learning unit "Finnish Forest" described above, I needed to choose one class to be a peer group for the group of the recently immigrated students. I was supervising one group and knew that it would be most convenient for me to run the intervention if I chose this group. The intervention was to take place during the multidisciplinary unit week and the supervisors were to work with their groups for the whole week. By choosing this particular group, I could combine my roles both as a teacher and a researcher in a practical way.

Yet, I had noticed last year that this group – being a music-specialised group – spent great efforts on making their presentations look and sound nice while paying less attention to the content and the language. Thus, I preferred to use the week with this class for rigorous academic work and ask some other teacher, some other group and some other researcher to participate in the intervention, for me to be able to set the students' needs first and concentrate on my task as a class supervisor. However, in the run-up to the intervention, there turned out to be increasing signs of tensions within this group between peer groups or individual students, like leaving someone out or speaking impolitely. In the Finnish National Core Curriculum, in addition to the subjects to be taught, seven "transversal competences" are pointed out that are to be promoted in school instruction as part of different subjects (Finnish National Agency of Education 2018). As important as competences in "thinking and learning to learn or multi-literacy", it is to rehearse "cultural competence, interaction and self-expression" (*ibid.*). While literacy skills can be practised throughout the year in any subject, the special week offered a special environment for studying interaction. Therefore, I changed my mind and chose my supervisees to participate in the intervention engaging non-verbal, embodied communication and collaboration. Of course, it is hard to say whether I found this justification only because I was looking for one. Reflecting on the case now, I still argue that I used my teacher knowledge and ethics appropriately, for a year later, in the annual discussions with every family, the students generally claimed that the mental atmosphere within the group was better than last year.

Observing critically, writing respectfully – questions of dissemination

"One form of ethnography is critical ethnography, studying issues like power and empowerment, inequality and inequity, dominance and repression, hegemony and victimization" (Creswell & Poth 2018: 94). However, critical examining of structures does not mean writing critically of individuals.

In my doctoral research (Nikkanen 2014), as mentioned above, I observed the process of a second-grade class with their teacher to write a song for the summer celebration of the school. They wrote lyrics, composed a melody, painted illustrations, planned instrumentation, agreed on task division and rehearsed for the performance. The process with a group of eight-year-old students, many with special educational needs, was not easy for the teacher to lead embodying values of participatory agency, collaboration and fair play. Having observed a process of balancing with educational ideals, curriculum objectives, musical relevance, time and space, my material contained data about some very sensitive moments.

In this case, it was easy for me to respect and even admire the solutions of the young teacher. Yet, while I brought the first drafts to our doctoral seminar, my peer candidates told they felt uneasy reading it and found themselves thinking of how they could help the teacher in the noisy mess. Having been present in the class and knowing the teacher, the students and the school, I also knew that the situation was not in fact out of the teacher's control as my peers had interpreted, although nurturing participatory agency may often look like a mess in the beginning. I spent a lot of time trying to find a way of writing so that I could catch the nature of the process from chaos to order and still keep the dignity of the teacher and guide the reader safely through the text.

In ethnography, it is necessary to also capture moments of chaos or conflict, but it is as necessary to write about these in a way that does not harm the persons or the community involved.

> Researchers should avoid any damage or harm to subjects that may be caused by research publications. However, this principle should not prevent the publication of research findings that may not be pleasing to subjects in all respects. A researcher's task is to produce new information without having to fear the reaction of authorities or other research subjects. Particularly research concerning the use of power and the functioning of social institutions must not be restricted on the grounds that results can have negative effects for subjects. The best way to ensure freedom of research is to conduct research carefully and systematically and to publish results with proper arguments and shedding light on different perspectives in a balanced manner.
>
> (TENK 2018)

It might be tempting to take sides when writing ethnography, for example, to sympathise with the students as much as to express antipathy towards the teachers. This kind of stance could even lure more readers. However, the researcher is committed to encounter all the participants with respect, even when writing about issues difficult to accept (see, e.g., Barbour 2010; Sikes 2010). This means looking at the issue from both sides; opening the view as to why such decisions are made or practices created; seeing the individual as members of their community and their decisions in relation to the culture of the field. Whilst critical ethnography aims at recognising irrelevant practices and structures and finally changing them, an ethical act is to discuss the problem while still in the field and, if possible, also to describe any progress happening. It is important to take into account the researcher's own part in the communication (see also Costley & Gibbs 2006: 95). When writing, instead of focusing on individual people, it may help to focus on processes. One solution is to describe the phenomenon, but not in detail, e.g., telling what happened but not who were the individual actors. It is important to keep the research questions at the forefront – how the practices, structures or professional understanding should be developed and how the problem could be solved.

Double agent – reflecting and balancing

The double role of teacher-researcher contains special ethical advantages as well as special ethical risks. Returning to Macfarlane's fears about the quality of the research conducted by an insider, I argue that, although acknowledging the risks as real, actually, the possibility to change the educational process is the clue of the double position as a teacher-researcher. However, constant critical reflection is needed for recognising one's multiple motifs for action.

Ideally, being a "double agent" and hence knowing the practices, languages and ethical codes of both professions, a teacher-researcher can act as an *active agent* for participatory practices and positive change in both fields. A teacher-researcher possesses timely knowledge on quickly changing school practices. The context-specific tacit knowledge that may be gained only by working in a school community may help to develop special, local, research-based pedagogical solutions, as well as relevant research designs. With professional researcher skills, in turn, these local solutions may be evaluated and reported to the benefit of global knowledge.

The ethical risks derive from balancing with these two roles. In my experience, the roles are not contradicting, but partly overlapping. Constant critical reflection is needed through all the phases (Guillemin & Gillam 2004: 274) and all the layers (Stutchbury & Fox: 2009) of research. First, ethical consideration is needed on the effects of sharing the time between two tasks and two employers; does it harm my school work that I work only 80 per cent at school? Is it possible to do any meaningful research with only 20 per cent weekly working time? On one hand, some of the work is overlapping, for example, part of planning and teaching in a course that is carried out also as a research intervention. On the other hand, both the school and the university have their demands concerning the duties outside of the actual teaching or researching, and they seem often to be the same for me as they are for the full-time teachers and researchers.

Second, there are issues of balancing duties as a member of two staffs. Does it harm the school community if I am present only four days a week? Does someone need to do extra work due to my absence? With so few working hours, do I harm communication in my research group? While a researcher from outside of the school can ask for permission to observe any place or class or group during a day, a teacher-researcher needs to follow both the schedules and the organisational structures of the school. Thus, the challenge is to keep your position as a normal member of the staff. For example, if you are a member of one team, it is difficult to follow or effect the work of other teams. Do the benefits of being a link between the two fields compensate for the shortage of time?

Ethical codes of both teachers and ethnographers are converging in the sense that everything that is not denied is not allowed either.

> In research in the humanities and social and behavioural sciences, ethical questions focus on the encounter between the researcher and the subject, which can include unanticipated factors. The researcher is always responsible for the ethical and moral solutions in a study.
>
> (TENK 2009: 13)

> The work of teaching should include consideration and evaluation of the ethics of one's own goals and motives.
>
> (OAJ 2018)

Thus, the third challenge is balancing the interest of collecting data and developing practices with ethical action as a teacher. Constant situational, critical and sensitive consideration one's own motives is needed for the double role; do I research to make the practice better, or do I change practice to make the research better? Do I research to develop practices that may also help my colleagues, or do I use my colleagues to help my research? Do I develop practices to make the courses better for my students, or do I use the students in developing my courses to make my research better? (See also Guillemin & Gillam 2004: 275.) While at best the whole school community may benefit from the professional skills of a teacher-researcher in developing the educational culture, at worst there is a danger of disintegrating the community. If the colleagues, students or parents feel insecure about the purposes or methods of the research, instead of being appreciated as an active agent, the teacher-researcher may be perceived as a *spy agent*. Thus, special sensibility is needed in choosing both the research topics and methods.

While an outsider may see or say something that would not be possible for an insider, sometimes it is also vice-versa. Andrew Barbour (2010), for example, describes a problematic situation while observing teaching of his colleague and friend. He noticed some obvious malpractice but felt unable to articulate it while an outsider in this particular classroom and feeling a need to be grateful for access to the field. While being part of the phenomenon researched also causes hindrances for some topics, methods and actions, it also allows the researcher to affect on practice from inside. If a practice is noticed to confront the public aims, an insider, as a full member of a community and as a peer, may take the initiative and articulate that *we* have something wrong here and suggest that *we* do something to this together.

Lizzi Milligan (2016) coins a term, *in-betweener*, in context to be a teacher doing ethnography in a foreign school and being in a position between students and the staff, and being an insider in school life but an outsider in the local culture. In this position Milligan found herself getting closer to the students than she would have if acting as a teacher. However, for some students she seemed to be "the outsider who can change their world" (p. 241). The researcher as an outsider may see and hear issues that are never questioned in the community, but have no power to change them other than pointing them out, whereas a teacher-researcher, as an insider in both the fields, is able to make research and practice interact immediately in one's own practice.

For me, the great chance of being able to work as a teacher-researcher in two great professional communities has also caused anxiety. There are sometimes amazing things happening and I catch myself thinking that there is no recording of these situations taking place. Simultaneously, I remind myself that there is no need. I can relax as a researcher and enjoy such moments in the role of a teacher, for this is not my research topic – but, as I find this fascinating professionally, it might become one in the future.

Note

1 The Finnish system of the National Core Curriculum with local applications is described as follows on the web page of the Finnish National Board for Education: "The national core curriculum is drawn up by the Finnish National Agency for Education. It includes the objectives and core contents of different subjects, as well as the principles of pupil assessment, special-needs education, pupil welfare and educational guidance". The principles of a good learning environment, working approaches as well as the concept of learning are also addressed in the core curriculum. The education providers, usually the local education authorities and the schools themselves draw up their own curricula for pre-primary and basic education within the framework of the national core curriculum. These curricula may be prepared for individual municipalities or institutions or include both sections. The national core curriculum for basic education was renewed in 2014, and the new curriculum has been implemented in schools from August 2016. www.oph.fi/english/curricula_and_qualifications/basic_education.

Acknowledgements

This publication has been undertaken as part of the ArtsEqual project, funded by the Academy of Finland's Strategic Research Council from its Equality in Society programme (project no. 293199).

References

Barbour, A. 2010. "Exploring some ethical dilemmas and obligations of the ethnographer". *Ethnography and Education* 5(2): 159–173.

Costley, C. and Gibbs, P. 2006. "Researching others: care as an ethic for practitioner researchers". *Studies in Higher Education* 31(1): 89–98.

Creswell, J.W. and Poth, C.N. 2018. *Qualitative Inquiry and Research Design: Choosing among Five Approaches*, 4th edn. Los Angeles, CA: SAGE.

Finnish National Agency of Education. 2018. *New National Core Curriculum for Basic Education*. www.oph.fi/english/curricula_and_qualifications/basic_education/curricula_2014#Transversal%20competences%20as%20part%20of%20every%20subject.

Guillemin, M. and Gillam, L. 2004. "Ethics, reflexivity, and 'ethically important moments' in research". *Qualitative Inquiry* 10(2): 261–280.

Gray, D.E. 2014. *Doing Research in the Real World*, 3rd edn. London: SAGE.

Hammersley, M. 2013. "Response 1 to 'generic ethics principles in social science research'". *Generic Ethics Principles in Social Science Research*. Professional Briefings (3): 6–8. London: Academy of Social Sciences. www.acss.org.uk/wp-content/uploads/2014/01/Professional-Briefings-3-Ethics-r.pdf.

Josselsson, R. 2007. "The ethical attitude in narrative research: principles and practicalities". In *Handbook of Narrative Inquiry: Mapping a Methodology*, edited by D. Jean Clandinin, 537–567. Thousand Oaks, CA: SAGE.

van Langenhove, L. and Harré, R. 1999. "Introducing positioning theory". In *Positioning Theory: Moral Contexts of Intentional Action*, edited by R. Harré and L. van Langenhove, 14–31. Oxford; Malden, MA: Blackwell.

Levinson, M.P. 2010. "Accountability to research participants: unresolved dilemmas and unravelling ethics". *Ethnography and Education* 5(2): 193–207.

MacDonald, S. 2017. "Embedded ethics and research integrity: a response to 'The Quest for Generic Ethics Principles in Social Science Research' by David Carpenter". In *Finding Common Ground: Consensus in Research Ethics Across the Social Sciences*, edited by R. Iphofen, 29–35. Advances in Research Ethics and Integrity 1. Emerald Publishing.

Macfarlane, B. 2009. *Researching with Integrity: The Ethics of Academic Enquiry*. New York: Routledge.

Milligan, L. 2016. "Insider-outsider-inbetweener? Researcher positioning, participative methods and cross-cultural educational research". *Compare: A Journal of Comparative and International Education* 46(2): 235–250.

Nichols, J. 2016. "Sharing the stage: ethical dimensions of narrative inquiry in music education". *Journal of Research in Music Education* 63(4): 439–454.

Nikkanen, H. 2010. "Developing democratic practices in a school community through musical performance". *Finnish Journal of Music Education*, Special Issue, *Revitalizing Traditions*, 13(2): 48–56.

Nikkanen, H.M. 2014. *Musiikkiesitykset ja juhlat koulun toimintakulttuurin rakentajina* [*Musical Performances and School Celebrations Constructing the Educational Culture of the School*]. Helsinki: Sibelius Academy of the University of Arts.

OAJ. 2018. *Ethical Principles for the Teaching Profession*. OAJ – The Trade Union of Education in Finland. www.oaj.fi/cs/oaj/Ethical%20Principles%20for%20the%20Teaching%20Profession_en.

Sikes, P. 2010. "Teacher–student sexual relations: key risks and ethical issues". *Ethnography and Education* 5(2): 143–157.

Stutchbury, K. and Fox, A. 2009. "Ethics in educational research: introducing a methodological tool for effective ethical analysis". *Cambridge Journal of Education* 39(4): 489–504.

Swedish Research Council. 2017. *Good Research Practice*. Stockholm: Swedish Research Council. www.vr.se/download/18.5639980c162791bbfe697882/1529480529472/Good-Research-Practice_VR_2017.pdf.

TENK. 2009. *Ethical Principles of Research in the Humanities and Social and Behavioural Sciences and Proposals for Ethical Review*. Finnish National Advisory Board on Research Ethics. www.tenk.fi/sites/tenk.fi/files/ethicalprinciples.pdf.

TENK. 2018. *Ethical Review in Human Sciences: Ethical Principles of Research in the Humanities and Social and Behavioural Sciences*. Finnish National Board on Research Integrity TENK. www.tenk.fi/en/ethical-review-in-human-sciences.

Chapter 7

Ethical reflections on critical ethnography

Marianne Dovemark

Introduction

This paper started out with my need to try to understand my reflexive and ethical positioning within my research as well as my professionalism (e.g. Barbour 2010). Studying the marketisation of the Swedish school system has for me been an interesting, important and actually also a frustrating business. The frustration has to do with how there is overwhelming research evidence that clearly points to an increasing injustice, segregation and inequality brought in to the society by a marketised school system, and yet how little this appears to affect politicians' perceptions about it and how it is an idea that has become taken for granted, rarely questioned any more (Dovemark 2017; Englund 2018).

Freedom of choice reforms have deepened prevailing segregation patterns, causing not only unequal but also segregated schools[1] that are contributing to an even more divided society (cf. SNAE 2012) with better conditions for already-well-off groups but worse conditions for many socially vulnerable groups (Englund 2018), and, of course, for new arrivals (Dovemark & Beach 2014, 2016, 2018). In Sweden today, the logic of parents with higher education and high incomes and/or with specific private and often self-esteemed expectations and interests requiring adjustment of a school to their children is actually seldom questioned. Children's schooling is now seen more as a pure family affair rather than as part of a common democracy project focusing on the civic role in the society (Englund 2018). The question is how the freedom of choosing a school can be understood in relation to equal opportunities, safety, quality and the possibility for all children to get a good education.

Results of this kind of research are important to forward to different stakeholders. However, in doing so, I have found a range of reactions and reflections. In this text my starting point will be discussions around reactions to my research from a special group, namely school and preschool leaders I have met during different lectures and seminars. During the last three years I have been involved in the obligatory (by the state) education of school and preschool leaders (from now on *school leaders*) in Sweden. All school leaders, regardless of whether they work for a public or private-owned school, have to complete the education. The aim of the programme is to strengthen school leaders' ability to lead and control their organisation (SNAE 2015). The Swedish National Agency for Education sets the scene and a number of universities are given the task to implement the programme on the basis of this framework. One of my tasks within the programme has been to present lectures about my research results within the course Objectives and Result Management.

One very clear pattern already appeared even at the first lecture; depending on whether the school leaders were employed in a public or free school/preschool they responded to my content in the lecture differently. The school leaders within free schools often became upset, sometimes angry or, even, furious and as a result a tense mood arose. I realised that my message provoked representatives from the private free school sector. I was accused of presenting untrue results. I found myself caught in a dilemma of being torn between disseminating the most important research results and knowing antagonising different stakeholders.

I was actually unprepared for this reaction. To me the lecture was about presenting research results, nothing else. I tried time after time, when meeting new groups of school leaders, to present the research results in different ways to reduce the annoyance and indignation, but without much success. While the public school leaders seemed to be quite satisfied (at least they did not show any anger and some even came up to me after the lecture to say thanks and offer affirmation of my results), my research results still antagonised school leaders from the private free school sector.

The reactions puzzled me, and again, as I had done during the entire research process, I wondered about the choices and representations I had made throughout the research process and what I presented in the end. Questions about gaining permission, about my own identity as a researcher, power relations and on what premises and by what right I was speaking about the studied context, popped up in my head. In this chapter I want to open up a critical discussion about the contextual nature of fieldwork, what affects our choices during the research process, and problematise the understanding of covert/overt research and informed consent.

Setting the scene

During the last decade we have been conducting research about the Swedish marketised school system. In Sweden today, there is a state-regulated school system where public and private actors play on a highly market-exposed quasi-market (Börjesson 2016; Lundahl 2002; Lundahl et al. 2014). Since the early 1990s, Sweden has created one of the world's most market-exposed school systems, rivaling those in Chile and New Zealand. One example is that we now have two listed education companies (AcadeMedia and the International English school) owned by private equity firms (Dovemark 2017). Seventy-five per cent of the private, free school students go to schools run as limited liability companies. Today, a third of upper-secondary schools are private, free schools and almost 20 per cent of compulsory schools (Economics Facts 2018), most of them within the three biggest companies, AcadeMedia, the International English school and the Knowledge School. The private companies' profit withdrawals are still sometimes openly discussed in Swedish media, while the issue of private actors in education is now taken for granted (Dovemark 2017).

The question we have highlighted within our research is how freedom of choice can be understood in relation to equal opportunities, safety, quality and the possibility for all children to get a good education. In our research we have been focusing: i) upon what grounds students make their choices (Dovemark & Holm 2015a, 2015b, 2018); ii) how different schools marketise themselves (Dovemark 2012, 2017; Dovemark & Lundström 2017); iii) through a Bernsteinian lens we have studied how the market creates schools with homogeneous identities (Bernstein 2000) through the way they call for (Althusser 1971/2008) different students; iv) how students are differentiated and positioned as different subjects (Fairclough 1992, 1995) to match the marketed programmes and created brands (Dovemark & Beach 2014, 2016, 2017; Dovemark & Erixon Arreman 2017; Erixon Arreman & Dovemark 2017); and v) how deregulation, privatisation and marketisation are deepening prevailing segregation patterns (Dovemark & Beach 2018; Dovemark et al. 2018). We have been doing observations and interviews in schools, open houses[2] and fairs,[3] analysing marketing materials, brochures and websites.

When conducting research at schools we got permission from school leaders, teachers and students to observe and interview. When visiting open houses and fairs as semi-public events I as a researcher could enter and get access to the field as any other visitor. When posing a question to a student, teacher or school leader, I presented myself as a researcher; however, when it came to the observations they were made without any real permissions and consent. I walked around at the fairs and at the school's open houses and took note of the information given to presumptive students and parents, posed questions, wrote field notes and so on. I noticed differences in teachers' and school leaders' appeal to parents and students, differences in number of parents and students visiting different schools' open houses and differences in how parents asked questions and about what. It soon turned out that schools were considered to have quite different status. In summary, I could quickly find that the distribution of education looked very different depending on how schools called for their students and the way schools marketised themselves. Obviously, this affected the way I as a critical ethnographer related to my data, and what assumptions and choices I made in the research process.

Critical research meets different stakeholders

In my attempts to meet and not annoy or upset the group of free school leaders, I soon realised that if I focused more on a micro level on students' school choices in relation to how they perceived their identities, the school leaders' reactions were quite different to the those when I presented results on a macro level in terms of extended and deepened segregation and differentiation. Quite quickly, though, I realised that to relate and to report research results only on a micro level was untenable and actually created serious conscience problems for me. To report results on reasons why students chose a particular school risked placing the blame on the individual student rather than on how the system is structured as a competitive market, where schools create their own brands positioning students as different subjects that students are more or less appealed to. In this way, homogeneous groups are created (Dovemark 2017; Dovemark & Holm 2015a, 2015b). The opposite became unavoidable – it became most important to present evidence about the unfairness the Swedish marketised system has added to and considerably extended to the education.

Accordingly, it became impossible not to explicitly express and set out policy and practical implications on what is happening in Sweden. As Gewirtz and Cribb (2006: 147) stress, "social research analyses may not *state* practical or policy implications but they do always to some degree *point* to them" (italics in original) and that means that as a researcher you have to "accept responsibility for the practical implications of their work" (147). I realised that I had to both face the anger I brought to some of the school leaders but above all, try to avoid the shame and guilt I felt when I did not clearly highlight the important results of inequalities, unfairness and unjust. I did not want to contribute with my research that obvious structural inequalities were transformed into questions of individual freedom of choice and identity. That would be most unethical for me. To grasp these dilemmas and try to understand the processes and my own reactions I started to read Gewirtz & Cribb's (2006, 2008) discussion with Hammersley (2006) about *ethical reflexivity*.

Ethical reflexivity

Ethnographers often face the question of ethics in at least two domains – the domain of interactions with the participants and the domain of representations of the participants (Dennis 2010). The basic ethical principles of undertaking ethnography include doing good (beneficence), avoiding doing harm (nonmaleficence) and protecting the autonomy, wellbeing, safety and dignity of all research participants. It means that I as an ethnographer should ensure that our research does not harm the safety, dignity or privacy of the people with whom we work or conduct research on. As an ethnographer you may strive to satisfy and attend to standardised ethical expectations mostly outlined by different institutional review boards that provide important limits and guidelines for the protection of human subjects in research (Dennis 2010: 123). These limits and guidelines are of course very important to guarantee that state and other financiers don't finance work that fails to respect human safety and integrity. But they can only do this to a certain extent.

By using concepts like *reflection* or *reflexivity* ethnographers talk and write about how a researcher takes an ethical position within the field practices. But, as Dennis (2010) points out, ethnographers often locate ethical decisions as internal to the research process itself, rather than as external and prior to the conduct of the research. Beach and Eriksson (2010: 130) point out that decisions of what is or is not ethical in research are often made inside ongoing research activities, "guided by first-hand experiences and influenced by commitments to scientific, ideological and political goals, beliefs and practices". They conclude that the researchers' worldviews and beliefs influence the interpretation of what was considered as ethical, rather than as a result of competing interests and values.

As an ethnographer, I am mainly involved in participant observations in which I, as a researcher, can observe people's actions and interactions as well as the larger contexts within which these take place. I can then open up a conversation with people about their observed actions and interactions. In other words, a lot of things are going on all the time. As a researcher taking field notes you cannot record every aspect of everyday life, you have to make your choices. Jeffrey (2018: 113) points out that "a major concern regarding observational notes written in the field relates to these field notes: whose reality do they represent, how is this reality portrayed, and who judges its validity?" The research is influenced by the fact that I myself am a part of the participatory observation and the conversation is shaped by what is happening at the moment together with what I as a researcher choose to select as a focus for further discussion (Wright Mills 1970). We can never overlook that the ethnographer is the analytical instrument. The ethnographer's "perspectives, analyses, and re-presentation are the main methodological instrument that carries out the research" (Jeffery 2018: 113). Writing an ethnography does not just mean that you must be aware that you are the main methodological instrument but includes the awareness that the entire research process constitutes of masses of choices and judgements. Realising all the evidence about the unfairness the Swedish marketised school system has added to and considerably extended to the education affects, of course every choice I make during the research process. Each obtained new knowledge creates new ethical questions and considerations that in turn generate new choices throughout the whole research process.

As many of the chapters in this book discuss, more ethical questions emerge than can be addressed through pre-study formal institutional reviews and, as Dennis (2010: 123) points out, "Behaving ethically in the field is a complex, dynamic endeavor". It is all about the integrity and awareness of the researcher or research team in the context of ethnography, the situations they create, the results they produce, the respect shown for the research subjects and so on. It is important to keep in mind that as a critical ethnographer my choices are about highlighting and giving voice to those who seldom get the opportunity to be heard. Implicit in this is that criticism will inevitably be directed towards a particular phenomenon, group etc.

Ethical guidelines from different science foundations often give concrete rules but, as these can be developed from different value positions, they are therefore likely to sometimes prove contradictory to one another and may challenge an individual's values and become problematic in practice. It is accepted that in societies like ours, humans are in practice not at all equal or even treated equally with equal rights and possibilities (Therborn 2018). Such knowledge makes it impossible to evade a researcher's philosophical position on research ethics. There is no *one* way of being ethical. There are different ways according to the foundational values of different ontological identities and practices within different moral philosophies of practice. Flinders (1992: 102) advocates the importance of "ethical literacy" and, as introduced in Chapter 1 and also referred to by other authors in this book (Chapters 3 and 8), introduced a framework which aimed to accept the diversity in ways of understanding the ethics of research and linked this to different ways of acting in accordance to that understanding.

Flinders' (1992) overview of his framework (see Table 1.3 in Chapter 1) highlights four ethical traditions: a) utilitarian, b) deontological, c) relational and d) ecological (Flinders 1992: 101). Flinders' main thesis is that each ethical framework is useful in highlighting the ethical foundations on which much of researchers' methodological work is built. The frameworks could help researchers to foresee ethical problems that turn up as research efforts unfold, and above all he wants to encourage researchers to think more deeply about the ethics of qualitative research.

Pedersen (2011: 72) takes the discussion of ethics of qualitative research a bit further when she applies the tools of post-humanist impulses to her critical animal study approach "(f)or political struggle – not to neutralize critique, but to reinvigorate and reinforce it" (see also Beach and Vigo Arrazola, Chapter 3, this volume). One and an important part of the researcher's responsibility lies in taking responsibility for addressing social injustice through socially responsible modes of communication. Pedersen's approach fits well into my own research and moral imperative to reveal a way of addressing the injustices and unfairness of the current marketised educational provision in relation to equal opportunities, safety, quality and the possibility for all children to get a good education. Research findings that would be highly unethical not to express and report.

Ethical reflexivity and critical ethnography

Being a critical ethnographer has implications. As a critical ethnographer I study issues like power and empowerment, inequality and inequity, dominance and repression, hegemony and victimisation and questions of values and judgements arise during the whole research process, from the very first idea about the focus to the final writing-up of the research.

As a critical ethnographer, my intention is to illustrate taken-for-granted activities and unfold how power is working within the studied area. My intention is to highlight and give voice to those who seldom get the opportunity to be heard.

Implicitly, it means that criticism is directed against a group that is rarely subjected to criticism or questioned. Nonetheless, there are questions that are likely to be challenging, and hence there are sensitivities needed to be considered by critical ethnographers to be answered and are of the highest importance to be studied. When posing critique there will of course be risks limiting my access to sites, people and data production possibilities, as in the case of how the school choice and opening up an educational market has added and considerably extended to the unfairness of provision of education in Sweden with increasing societal gaps. The school leaders from the free school sector I met during my lectures are of course most likely to be challenged by my research, many of them leading effective pre/ schools with a maximum application rate of children and students.

But when we find that there are many effective and popular free schools, we also have to take into consideration that the geography of the school market clearly shows that free schools are mainly established in major cities and in metropolitan areas (Beach & Dovemark forthcoming; Fjellman 2017; Yang Hansen & Gustafsson 2016). Another eye-catching fact, as was noted in *Teachers' Magazine* (17 October 2016), based on a survey done by one of the teacher unions shows that in 70 per cent of Sweden's municipalities, the proportion of pupils with a foreign background is higher in the municipality's own schools than in the private free schools in the municipality and the difference is even more pronounced when looking at parents' educational level. In 86 per cent of the municipalities, the proportion of students with university-educated parents is higher in the private free schools than in the public schools (*Teachers' Magazine* 2016). Thus, there is a clear pattern in relation to free schools that can be termed as positive segregation (Bunar & Ambrose 2018; Forsberg 2018). Research results pointing to societal system problems can of course be considered as challenging for those who have an opportunity to take advantages of the system as the private free schools.

Nonetheless, questions must be: what kind of representations are made? What kind of issues can be raised when applied to researching in the range of research settings such as classrooms, public crowds or semi-public events that I have found myself studying? Do I give a fair picture of what is going on? What statements can I make from my research in semi-public areas where I have not really asked for permission or have informed consent? Can I be considered as dealing with concealment of my research? These questions all popped into my head when I was accused of being dishonest and unfair. To grasp questions like these, I want to put light on and problematise the question of informed consent and concealment within ethnography.

Ethical reflexivity and the question of informed consent

When doing any research, we primarily raise the importance of informed consent, avoidance of harm and confidentiality. Concealment, for example within ethnography, is often considered ethically problematic due to normative practices, seen by many institutional review boards as a necessity, to gain informed consent when getting permission prior to conducting research. Covert methods are often seen as forms of civil betrayal that violate the rights of an individual not to be studied and are often treated as an antithesis to open and overt research (Lugosi 2006: 542), which actually can be considered as quite ironic as long as the workings of power and ideology are not mentioned. Too strong a focus on openness or not can be misleading as there are many other dimensions of differences in ethnography that are at least as challenging (and may be also far more ethically problematic). The question I propose: is there a clear division between overt and covert research? Or is that even *the issue?*

Voluntary participation is taken for granted and gaining informed consent has become an established standard practice linked to the discourse of human rights and autonomy (Corrigan 2003). This of course matches the aims of ethnographers who strive to be as open and transparent as possible about their purpose and intentions. When taking a critical starting point though, I have found that even normative practices can and need to be called into question, as possibly the most appropriate way to act in particular circumstances, when held up against personal values and judgements about how to conduct any particular study. Questions of whether we have moral obligations vis-à-vis people involved in our research are questions we need to ask ourselves, questions that need to be posed in the wake of challenges to the society (Pedersen 2011). This cannot be automatically dismissed as a normative practice or argument but rather as a position from a methodological perspective. Critique is needed in order to clarify the disadvantages and shortcomings the marketisation of the education system is creating. That is why the question of what is ethically right or wrong when addressing how freedom of choice can be understood in relation to equal opportunities, safety, quality and the possibility for all children to get a good education is an open question and should always appear throughout the whole research process.

Reading Gewirtz and Cribb (2006, 2008) made me rethink contemporary ethical discussions of research. Flinders (1992: 108) stresses the importance to view the world in terms of unified systems when focusing on what he calls an *ecological ethical framework.* "Ecological" does not refer to an environment per se, but to "a set of independent relationships" (108). Classrooms, for example, are what Flinders calls "biotic environments", filled with the lives of pupils and teachers, a cultural milieu populated by language, relationships and ideas: "These cultural dimensions of the classroom – its curriculum and norms of interaction – are what connect it meaningfully with the world beyond its four walls" (108). Accordingly, when researching the Swedish marketised educational system we cannot just focus on students' own choices and identities. That would be unethical. We have to pull in the entire ecological web of factors that directly affects the outcome of the education system. We have to bring in the whole system of public and private free schools, what different programmes different schools offer, how to fund students' education, opportunities for profit, what constructions of student subjects different schools call for in their market materials, what locations the schools have, how teachers, school leaders and students talk about different schools and programmes, what status different schools have etc. We have to call for the biotic environment to bring justice to the studied area. Not to do so would be unethical.

Reflexivity as social and ethical relationships

Referring to Bateson (1972, in Flinders 1992: 108) states that "mental processes are never bottled up inside a person's head but are equally 'inside' all of the shared information pathways (e.g., language and forms of nonverbal communication) that constitute a culture". That means, as I mentioned above, that my personal involvement in social and fieldwork relations also shape my data production, analyses and writing (cf. Jeffrey 2018). When trying to structure the ability to judge my own research activities as ethical or not in developing relationships with participants during my fieldwork, I must highlight, question and face dilemmas concerning my own ontological identity and moral philosophy. During my different studies within the marketised Swedish school system I have found myself several times caught up in frustration and dilemmas due to what the system has added and extended to the increasing inequalities in the society in relation to equal opportunities, safety, quality and the possibility for all children to get a good education. This frustration has of course influenced me in my continuing choices in the research process which still generates ethical reflexivity in an ongoing process.

Moreover, by talking about *ethical reflexivity* I emphasise that it is not only my social relationships in the field that shape the direction and products of my research but also my ontological identity and moral philosophy. This does not mean that an account of the world produced by me as a researcher simply reflects my personal and social characteristics. Ethical reflexivity, according to Gewirtz and Cribb (2006: 153), is not a manifestation of a person-relative conception of knowledge but rather "a dimension of rigor in the context of a realist conception of knowledge". Ethical reflexivity encompasses several elements. To gain such rigor I use Gewirtz and Cribb's (2006: 148) elements of reflexivity to help make thoughtful choices throughout the research process. This involved the choice of research field, through the production of data, analysis and wrapping up; for each project this involved considering, the political context and implications of my work.

Going back to my research field, the marketised Swedish education system, there will of course be values that are known to be contentious and controversial and in need of clarification and justification. As a result of the ethically reflexive stance I took as well as my methodological position as a critical ethnographer, I strove to scrutinise and make explicit my value commitments through my chosen theoretical framework while, at the same time, trying to make explicit the taken-for-granted worldview I am inhabiting. This position means that I have to be prepared to develop my value judgements in a way that is responsive to those dilemmas faced by those operating in the social context being studied (Gewirtz & Cribb 2006). When I was accused of presenting untrue results I became unsure about my relations to inter alia informed consent and concealment which I now can see is a inevitable part of fieldwork.

Ethical frameworks as ontological identities and moral philosophy

The question is whether the ethical criteria such as informed consent different institutional review boards provide become both taken for granted and instrumental in a way that we forget deeper ethical frameworks as our ontological identities and moral philosophy. All research appraisal criteria have an opt-out clause on the demand for informed consent. Can research that has not been based on informed consent, as my own research in semi-public areas as open houses and fairs, be considered to meet ethical standards or not? Was I unfair in presenting the research results in the way I did? Was it unethical to interfere with participants as students and parents who had an essentially different purpose than mine in visiting the open houses and fairs? Was my presence and study to be considered as covert research per se? In line with Spicker (2011: 120) I argue that fieldwork relationships inevitably involve some covertness and limiting disclosure which are both practical and methodological. It is both an unavoidable and often an inevitable part of fieldwork (Lugosi 2006: 542), even though it is seldom discussed when writing up an ethnography (Beach & Eriksson 2010).

I argue that overt research always has covert elements (cf. Lugosi 2006). Ethnographic research always by design is liable to include processes that cannot be planned and these processes are situational (Levinson 2010). As has been discussed in this chapter already, as a researcher you are "engaged in making evaluative and political judgements and choices" (Gewirtz & Cribb 2006: 142) all the time beyond the importance of being descriptive and explanatory. Research will always have political commitments in one way or another regardless of whether it is considered to be overt or covert, if you want it or not.

We all should be aware of the effect of our ontological identities and moral philosophy on the decisions and choices concerning which data to produce, the wording of the survey, the organisation of the data, the sample and so on. When I am doing my observations and interviews, I am already marinated as with the knowledge of distribution of profits to the shareholders of the companies presenting their schools at the fair or in the schools I visit. I also have knowledge, which was noted in *Teachers' Magazine* (5 October 2018), of how these profits can be achieved through fewer teachers, lower teacher salaries (at least in profit-making independent schools) and a large proportion of students with highly educated parents (*Teachers' Magazine* 2018). Being aware of this knowledge affects my perception. My ontological identity and moral philosophy are pending and present all the time. It creates the necessity for essential reflexivity. Once again, in addition to the data, values permeate all other aspects of research: analysis, choice of constructs used to lump data together, deciding which "findings" to present and the ways in which the data and analyses are represented, interpreted and explained. Surely, we all worry about these processes; worried of becoming dishonest, becoming embedded in a strongly ideological bias that affects the validity of the research and its representations. The desire and quest to be transparent has to be the goal in this process but at the same time as a researcher taking a critical standpoint you got responsibility for addressing social injustice through socially responsible modes of communication (Pedersen 2011).

Discussion and conclusion

When I was accused of presenting untrue results and found myself caught in a dilemma of being torn between disseminating the most important research results and knowingly antagonising different stakeholders I started to examine myself again about different considerations I had made during the research process.

As a researcher you make a lot of choices (Jeffrey 2018) depending on your values and you need to deal with ethical dilemmas based on these choices. These choices must of course become transparent for the reader. Questions like: what focus does your research have? What kind of questions do you pose in a questionnaire or in an interview? What is your focus during observations? Where do you place your emphasis in your analysis? must be set throughout the entire research process. Choices involve all parts of your research process: choice of field, producing data, analysing data and writing up data. Whatever the choices are, the choices have "implications for the way in which the responsibility for the problem is constructed and thereby has political implications" (Gewirtz & Cribb 2006: 143). As Beach and Eriksson (2010: 135) stress referring to Gudmundsdottir (1990) "*ethical positions are value committed* and concern the establishment of a way of being for oneself and a crafting of relations to other individuals and groups in which these values can be reflected and lived out in research practices" (italics in original).

What I claim in this chapter is that politically committed research is not incompatible with academic rigor. On the contrary, to raise ethical dilemmas in relation to your ontological identity and moral philosophy is part of academic rigidity beside the production of knowledge. But of course, a researcher must be self-conscious about the way in which their value judgements shape their research (cf. Gewirtz & Cribb 2006). As a researcher I am part of the world I research, and that very fact involves countless ethical and political choices as a citizen and as a researcher. The knowledge I have and am producing does and will affect me both as a citizen and as a researcher. To ignore this would be a lie to both myself and my readers. However, I as a researcher have to be aware that varied typographies of power, knowledge and emerging inter/subjectivities carry not only theoretical, but *political* significance. The answer to the question as to whether anybody benefits from my research can be answered: as a critical ethnographer my aim is to try to raise the voices of those to whom life is a constant struggle often with suffering imposed by others. However, for those who seldom experience oppression, the knowledge I produce may be seen as provocative and even considered unfair. These thoughts might explain what made some of the school leaders so upset about my lectures.

As a researcher you can rely on an explanation of your choice of theoretical framework as a way to be transparent for the reader. I clarify, as a critical ethnographer, what theories I use. When using theories that are in line with a criticism of the society, I am aware that I focus on some parts, rather than others, in the researched field. I do take into consideration the power structures but by prioritising the need to focus on those people whose voices are usually not heard. Of course, I cannot expect that school leaders will respond well to this knowledge. Consequently, to them, many of my results are outrageous. To fully hear the findings, they would need to take a critical stance themselves and be prepared to challenge the status quo and assumptions within their own worldview.

In retrospect, I should not change the content of my lectures to avoid upsetting the emotions of the powerful. The results should be presented to them and de facto the most appropriate course should actually be to leave the reaction with the audience and try to ignore it.

The injustice we discover in the market-oriented education system is a fact that not only needs to be written in a number of research articles, but, above all, the effects should be disclosed to those directly affected by them. I argue that to be silent about that is to behave unethically as a researcher.

As has been shown in this chapter, researching a politically "hot" area has its implications. The debate gets easily polarised and reported research findings are sometimes interpreted as if you as a researcher have your own agenda or want to hide something. When I was accused of being dishonest and unfair, I became unsure and began to wonder over questions about informed consent and concealment. Reading Gewirtz and Cribb (2006, 2008) made me rethink contemporary ethical discussions of research. The critical ethnography that I practice is unashamedly "consistent and committed critical attention to any oppressive institutions, arrangements, and practices that regulate and exploit the life conditions of humans and nonhumans alike" (Pedersen 2011: 78). This offers a moral imperative to find a way of addressing the injustices and unfairness that the current marketised educational provision adds to the injustices already embedded in society.

Ethical reflexivity requires that I as a researcher make explicit my reflections of ontological identity and moral philosophy as a way of indicating the socially constructed nature of the research process in my studies and the partiality and contingency of my research accounts. To do this is an attempt to justify both the value positions that are adopted and the feasibilities and practicalities of realising the alternative, more desirable, possible worlds that are implied in those value positions. To do this is a way to try to avoid pitfalls of naive neutrality. I as a researcher have to be aware of my research's possible implications on the activities I study. I should not be content with solely supplying facts and knowledge considering there always is a relation between knowledge production and knowledge use. I have argued in this chapter that this is a way of carrying out rigorous research informed by a commitment to bringing about social and political change, although there can be a number of hazards on that path. Rigour, honesty, fairness, sense and significance must be there. Not to do so is to be considered unethical.

Notes

1 The school was already massively uneven even if there was an expressed ambition for some degree of parity (SOU 1990: 44). Marketisation and privatisation, though, had made things significantly worse.
2 Most Swedish upper-secondary schools invite presumptive students and parents to their open houses, where they present their pedagogic organisation. These events are often on evenings and/or weekends.
3 Most bigger cities organise a fair each year, where future students and parents can choose between different schools' selection of education. Here, both public and private education is represented. Large equity firms, such as AcadeMedia, sell education alongside public alternatives or single foundation-owned schools.

References

Barbour, A. 2010. "Exploring some ethical dilemmas and obligations of the ethnographer". *Ethnography and Education* 5(2): 159–173.

Bateson, G. 1972. *Steps to an Ecology of Mind*, New York: Ballantine.

Beach, D. and Dovemark, M. forthcoming. "Equity and choice for newly arrived migrants". In *Neoliberalism and Market Forces in Education: Lessons from Sweden*, edited by M. Dahlstedt and A. Fejes. London: Routledge.

Beach, D. and Eriksson, A. 2010. "The relationships between ethical positions and methodological approaches: a Scandinavian perspective". *Ethnography and Education* 5(2): 129–142.

Bernstein, B. 2000. *Pedagogy, Symbolic Control and Identity: Theory, Research, Critique*. Lanham, MD: Rowman & Littlefield.

Börjesson, M. 2016. *Från Likvärdighet Till Marknad: En Studie av Offentligt och Privat Inflytande över Skolans Styrning i Svensk Utbildningspolitik 1969–1999* [*From Equity to Market: A Study of Public and Private Influence of School's Governance in Swedish Education Policy 1969–1999*]. Örebro: Örebro Studies in Education 52.

Bunar, N. and Ambrose, A. 2018. "Urban polarisering och marknadens förlorare" [Urban polarization and the market's losers]. In *Skolan, Marknaden och framtiden* [*The School, the Market and the Future*], edited by M. Dahlstedt and A. Fejes, 169–186. Lund: Studentlitteratur.

Corrigan, O. 2003. "Empty ethics: The problem with informed consent". *Sociology of Health and Illness* 25(3): 768–792.

Dennis, B. 2010. "Ethical dilemmas in the field: the complex nature of doing education ethnography". *Ethnography and Education* 5(2): 123–127.

Dovemark, M. 2012. "Yrkesval eller utsortering?" [Professional choice or being sort out?] In *Lärare och lärande I yrkesprogram och introduktionsprogram* [*Teachers and Learning in*

Vocational Programmes and Introductory Programmes], edited by I.H. Loeb and H. Korp, 75–94. Lund: Studentlitteratur.

Dovemark, M. 2017. "Utbildning till salu – konkurrens differentiering och varumärke. Tema nummer" [Education for sale – competition, differentiation and brands]. *Utbildning & Demokrati* [*Education & Democracy*] 26(1): 67–86.

Dovemark, M. and Beach, D. 2014. "Academic work on a back-burner: habituating students in the upper-secondary school towards marginality and a life in the precariat". *International Journal of Inclusive Education* 19(6): 583–594.

Dovemark, M. and Beach, D. 2016. "From learning to labour to learning for precarity". *Ethnography and Education* 11(2): 174–188.

Dovemark, M. and Beach, D. 2018. "Skolan, marknaden och prekariatet" [The school, the market and the precariat]. In *Skolan, Marknaden och framtiden* [*The School, the Market and the Future*], edited by M. Dahlstedt and A. Fejes, 187–202. Lund: Studentlitteratur.

Dovemark, M. and Erixon Arreman, I. 2017. "The implications of school marketisation for students enrolled on introductory programmes in Swedish upper secondary education". *Education, Citizenship and Social Justice* 12(1): 49–62.

Dovemark, M. and Holm, A.-S. 2015a. "Pedagogic identities for sale! Segregation and homogenization in Swedish upper secondary school". *British Journal of Sociology of Education* 38(4): 518–532.

Dovemark, M. and Holm, A.-S. 2015b. "Förortens skola – Möjligheternas skola?" [Schools in the suburb-the schools of possibilities?] *Utbildning och lärande* [*Education and learning*] 9(1): 62–78.

Dovemark, M. and Lundström, U. 2017. "Skolan och marknaden" [The school and the market]. *Utbildning & Demokrati* [*Democarcy & Education*], 61(1): 5–18.

Dovemark, M., Kosonen, S., Kauko, J., Hansen, P., Magnúsdóttir, B. and Rasmussen, A. 2018. "Deregulation, privatisation, and marketisation of Nordic comprehensive education: social changes reflected in schooling". *Education and Inquiry* 9(1): 122–142.

Economics Facts. 2018. www.ekonomifakta.se/Fakta/Valfarden-i-privat-regi/Skolan-i-privat-regi/Antal-friskolor-i-Sverige/.

Englund, T. 2018. "Är demokratin hotad? Om private intressen och skolans mvandling" [Is democracy threatened? About private interests and schools' transformation]. *Utbildning & Demokrati* [*Education & Democracy*] 28(1): 115–135.

Erixon Arreman, I. and Dovemark, M. 2017. "Social justice in Swedish post-16 education? New preparatory programmes". *Scandinavian Journal of Educational Research* 62(4): 570–585.

Fairclough, N. 1989. *Language and Power*. London: Longman.

Fairclough, N. 1992. *Discourse and Social Change*. Cambridge: Polity Press.

Fjellman, A.-M. 2017. "Differentiering genom reglerad marknadsanpassning – uppkomsten av en regional skolmarknad" [Differentiation through regulated market adaptation – the emergence of a regional school market]. *Utbilding & Demokrati* [*Education & Democracy*] 1(26): 107–132.

Flinders, D.J. 1992. "In search of ethical guidance: constructing a basis for dialogue". *Qualitative Studies in Education* 5(2): 101–115.

Forsberg, H. 2018. "Gymnasieval och segregation" [Upper-secondary school choice and segregation]. In *Skolan, Marknaden och framtiden* [*The School, the Market and the Future*], edited by M. Dahlstedt and A. Fejes, 203–226. Lund: Studentlitteratur.

Gewirtz, S. and Cribb, A. 2006. "What to do about values in social research: the case for ethical reflexivity in the sociology of education". *British Journal of Sociology of Education* 27(2): 141–155.

Gewirtz, S. and Cribb, A. 2008. "Differing to agree: a reply to Hammersley and Abraham". *British Journal of Sociology of Education* 29(5): 559–562.

Gudmundsdottir, S. 1990. "Values in pedagogical content knowledge". *Journal of Teacher Education* 41(3): 4452.

Hammersley, M. 2006. "Ethnography: problems and prospects". *Ethnography and Education* 1(1): 3–14.

Jeffrey, B. 2018. "Ethnografic writing". In *The Wiley Handbook of Ethnography of Education*, edited by D. Beach, C. Bagley and S. Marques Da Silva, 113–134. New York: John Wiley & Sons.

Levinson, M.P. 2010. "Accountability to research participants: unresolved dilemmas and unravelling ethics". *Ethnography and Education* 5(2): 193–207

Lugosi, P. 2006. "Between overt and covert research: concealment and disclosure in an ethnographic study of commercial hospitality". *Qualitative Inquiry* 12(3): 541–561.

Lundahl, L. 2002. "Sweden: decentralisation, deregulation, quasi-markets – and then what?" *Journal of Education Policy* 17(4): 687–697.

Lundahl, L., Erixon Arreman, I., Holm, A.-S. and Lundström, U. 2014. *Gymnasiet som marknad [Upper-secondary School as a Market]*. Umeå: Boréa.

Pedersen, H. 2011. "Release the moths: critical animal studies and the posthumanist impulse". *Culture, Theory and Critique* 52(1): 65–81.

SNAE. 2012. *Likvärdig utbildning i svensk grundskola? En kvantitativ analys av likvärdighet över tid [Equivalent Education in Swedish Primary School? A Quantitative Analysis of Equality Over Time]*. The Swedish National Agency for Education, Report 374. Stockholm: Fritzes.

SNAE. 2015. *The National School Leadership Training Programme. Goal document 2015–2021*. Stockholm: Fritzes.

SOU. 1990. *Demokrati och Makt i Sverige. Maktutredningens huvudrapport [Democracy and Power in Sweden. The Power Investigation's Main Report]*. Stockholm: Government Offices.

Spicker, P. 2011. "Ethical covert research". *Sociology* 45(1): 118–133.

Teachers' Magazine. 2016. https://lararnastidning.se/barn-till-hogutbildade-samlas-pa-friskolor/.

Teachers' Magazine. 2018. https://lararnastidning.se/lagst-larartathet-i-friskolekoncerner/.

Therborn, G. 2018. *Kapialet, överheten och alla andra. Klassamhället i Sverige – det radande och det kommande [The Capital, the Authority and Everyone Else. Class Society in Sweden – the Present and the Future]*. Lund: Arkiv Förlag.

Yang Hansen, K. and Gustafsson, J.-E. 2016. "Causes of educational segregation in Sweden – school choice or residential segregation". *Educational Research and Evaluation* 22(1–2): 23–44.

Wright Mills, C. 1970. *The Sociological Imagination*. Harmondsworth: Penguin.

Chapter 8

Ethical learning from an educational ethnography

The application of an ethical framework in doctoral supervision

Alison Fox and Rafael Mitchell

Introduction

This chapter operationalises Gewirtz and Cribb's (2006) call for an "ethically reflexive sociology of education" (147) in the context of doctoral research at an Ethiopian school. The doctoral study (undertaken by Rafael) applied an ethical appraisal framework developed by Alison and a colleague (Stutchbury & Fox 2009) for use in educational research. The framework is presented, through an empirical study, as a device to scaffold dialogic spaces within doctoral study for mutual learning through ethical reflexivity. This fills a gap in both the doctoral and ethical research bodies of literature. The chapter illustrates how a doctoral researcher and supervisor can learn together about what should constitute ethical ethnographic research in a particular context and with a particular researcher positionality.

The doctoral study was carried out in Tigray, Ethiopia, which saw both researchers exploring how this framework, developed from Western traditions of ethical thinking, could be applied to research in a sub-Saharan African setting. The purpose of the doctoral study was to develop knowledge-for-understanding (Wallace & Poulson 2003) about the perspectives, interests and agendas of different actors in the school, and the priorities reflected in routine activities and school-level decisions (Mitchell 2017a, 2017b, 2017c). Rafael had previously spent two years working in the education system in Tigray for Voluntary Service Overseas (VSO), which allowed him to bring relevant local (Ethiopian) experience, knowledge and contacts to discussions with the supervisory team (Mustajoki & Mustajoki 2017). Hence Rafael's positionality was not one of a total "outsider" to the context (Milligan 2016). Rafael led negotiations with those in the research setting during his probation period, using his growing situated knowledge to inform his case to the university's ethical review board (ERB). However, he came to recognise the limitations of his knowledge, having had no prior experience of conducting ethnography in Ethiopia, and remaining in many ways an "outsider" (Milligan 2016). The fieldwork was carried out through two extended periods of ethnographic participant observation in the school.

The chapter presents joint reflections on how extended dialogue throughout the doctoral journey allowed both researchers, through application of the ethical framework, to apply their values and experiences towards changes in understanding. This led to a new conceptualisation of the relationship between dimensions of the CERD framework and a practical application of Aristotelian views of virtue ethics.

The ethically reflexive dialogue sees Alison guiding Rafael as a "virtuous researcher" in terms of Aristotle's Doctrine of the Mean, enacting her vision to help Rafael consider his individual duty to follow a virtuous path between the vices of excess and deficit (Carpenter 2013; Macfarlane 2010). (See Figure 8.1.)

The framework at the heart of the approach presented offers four "dimensions" of ethical thinking (Stutchbury & Fox 2009). Use of the framework since its first publication has indicated that these dimensions can be usefully approached in a particular order reflected in the acronym "CERD".

Consequential thinking – the C of CERD – grew out of utilitarianism, with its aspiration for determining the best outcomes for society, into a moral philosophical way of thinking about the criteria for evaluating the benefits of one outcome over another (Scheffler 1988; Driver 2011). This relates to judging an act (in this case, related to research activites) by balancing its positive and negative consequences (Reynolds 1979). Consequential thinking is useful as both a starting point (to identify potential or wished-for outcomes of a study), and as an end point (to evaluate a study against these aspirations from the perspective of increased knowledge gained through the course of the research). *Consequential thinking* starts the process of identifying the moral drivers behind the study, in terms of anticipated benefits and intentions to minimise harm, through *ecological thinking*, which identifies all those associated with the study to whom

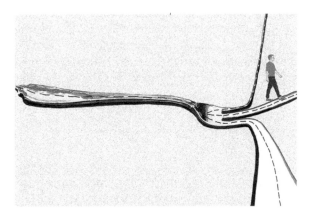

Figure 8.1 Navigating an Aristotelian path of virtue, rather than vice, in ethical research

Source: with permission of Alex Fox

consequential thinking needs to be applied, to *relational thinking*, as an application of the intentions to minimise harm and maximise benefits through showing respect and an "ethic of care" (Gilligan 2011; Noddings 1984) to use *deontological thinking*, to conclude a set of realisations as to the obligations a researcher feels they have, to whom and why.

Ecological thinking (Flinders 1992[1]) – the E of CERD – relates to the web of rules and expectations that surround and impinge on a study due to its situated nature. It includes legal and professional codes as well as the concerns of relevant sponsors and institutions. In Rafael's doctoral study there were two national contexts to consider due to the UK base of Rafael's university and the Ethiopian setting of the research site.

Relational thinking – the R of CERD – derives from feminist traditions and ethical thinking grounded in an "ethic of care" (Gilligan 2011; Noddings 1984), in which the "derivation and authority of moral behavior [*sic*] [comes] not in rules and obligations as such, but in our attachments and regard for others" (Flinders 1992: 106). This view prioritises the development of relationships and mutual learning through listening and giving voice to those involved in research. The nature of interpersonal relationships reflects the credibility of a study, as "trustworthiness should also be judged by how well the researcher got the Relational matters right" (Rossman & Rallis 2010: 382).

Deontological thinking – the D of CERD – draws on ethical traditions relating to meeting obligations. "Deontology", which derives from *deon* ("duty" in ancient Greek), applies to thinking which views decisions from the perspective of the duties of a moral agent. These duties indicate what is morally required and permissible in a particular society and are usually normative to that society. In this study Rafael and Alison sought to understand "to whom" and "in what ways" Rafael had obligations, by reviewing and balancing competing norms.

While some (e.g., Flinders 1992) consider ethical traditions such as these to be alternative research stances, Seedhouse (1998), writing in a healthcare context, proposed that it is ethical to view a study through multiple lenses, recognising "each idea is connected to others and it is difficult to be logical, consistent and sure that everything has been covered" (Stutchbury & Fox 2009: 503) without such scaffolding.

Methodology

Spaces were created within a doctoral supervisor–supervisee relationship that enabled Alison and Rafael to focus on the ethical aspects of his study. Six discussions of between ten and seventy-five minutes were held over a four-year period during the probation, fieldwork and pre-viva periods in parallel to the usual tutorials/supervisions. This chapter is based on an analysis of the dialogue between Alison and Rafael, not only during these recorded discussions but also through the course of the collaborative analysis involved in drafting this chapter.

An interpretative analytical approach was applied to the dataset (see Table 8.1) as an iterative process. The analysis is presented according to the four dimensions of the CERD framework (consequential, ecological, relational and deontological ethical thinking) reflecting on the probation; fieldwork; writing-up and post-viva phases of the study. This is a form of "constructive interpretation" (Chang 2016): interpretation, as Rafael and Alison's personal values and perspectives were drawn on throughout; and constructive, acknowledging how they were transformed through the process. "Autoethnographic writings interweave stories from the past with on-going self-discovery" (Chang 2016: 140) and this chapter charts how Alison and Rafael have been affected by each other's journeys.

The questions included in the original ethical appraisal framework (Stutchbury & Fox 2009) were used by Rafael in preparation for the recorded sessions A–F and referred to during the discussions. The four dimensions of the framework therefore informed the process of data collection and were also deductively applied to the ethical discussion transcripts to identify and "chunk" sections of dialogue for the analysis presented in this chapter. Separate documents were generated for each dimension, which were explored inductively using open coding. Through an iterative process, with either Alison or Rafael taking the lead, the codes for each dimension were conflated, refined or cut. Following agreement on a complete set of codes, conceptual connections were made between them. The codes were clustered and parent and sibling relationships agreed. The analysis was then reworked by reviewing each phase through the lens of the four dimensions.

The ethical reflexivity undertaken by Alison and Rafael applied Gewirtz and Cribb's (2006) recommendations, paraphrased below.

1   Being explicit about the value assumptions and evaluative judgements that inform or are embedded in every stage of our research.
2   Being prepared to offer a defence of our assumptions and judgements, to the extent that they might not be shared by others.

Table 8.1 Dataset on which this chapter is based

Data source	Dates	Notes
Ethical discussion A	January 2013	Audio (58 min) and transcript
Ethical discussion B	February 2013	Audio (79 min) and transcript
Ethical discussion C	September 2013	Audio (10 min) and transcript
Ethical discussion D	September 2014	Audio (75 min) and transcript
Ethical discussion E	January 2015	Audio (58 min) and transcript
Ethical discussion F	February 2016	Audio (67 min) and transcript
Collaborative Word documents for ECER 2017 conference	March–July 2017	Analysis of ethical discussions A–F, fieldnotes and synthesis leading to ECER 2017 conference paper
Collaborative Word documents	September 2017–April 2018	Analysis of ethical discussions A–F, memos, comments, emails and concept maps

3   Acknowledging, and where possible responding to, tensions between the various values that are embedded in our research.
4   Taking seriously the practical judgements and dilemmas of research participants.
5   Taking responsibility for the political and ethical implications of the research.

(147–148)

It was the case that Alison presented Rafael with a particular framework for ethical appraisal, sets of questions to explore the framework and created the spaces (in terms of time and location) in which to discuss the issues arising. The framework, however, is not a prescriptive tool and, as demonstrated, was subjected to critique by Rafael and further development. The recognition of Alison and Rafael's values, former experiences and agendas – in essence the complex reification of different cultural experiences that both brought as individuals – became a vital resource for ethical reflexivity. This approach allowed the tensions and practical decision-making related to the doctoral study to be made explicit.

Key findings

The outcomes of the analytic process detailed below (Table 8.2) are presented across three main phases of the doctoral study: probation; fieldwork and writing-up; post-viva. This analysis offers a window onto the shifting issues of significance along the doctoral journey, as well as unpacking the specific issues associated with ethical research in this particular research study: in Tigray, Ethiopia (as context) and by an outsider researcher with some prior experience of working in the Ethiopian school context (as positionality).

Consequential ethical thinking

Early in the probation period, thinking about who might be the beneficiaries of a study of an Ethiopian school (CE) led us to the question: who decides what is beneficial? (CF). The source of coded data is displayed in parentheses, e.g. (CR), where C refers to the dimension and R to a particular ethical discussion "chunk". Dates refer to post-viva memos associated with a particular data chunk. In cross-cultural research it is important to air assumptions and beliefs about who is generating knowledge and for whom, as well as acknowledging differences between the perceived and actual value of a study (Hett & Hett 2013). Returning to these issues after thinking ecologically helped Rafael to realise that planning for quality was an ethical issue. He concluded that consequential ethical thinking is not value-neutral, and requires a full appreciation of the study's context (CE), as consequences are always "in the service of something else, such as perceived responsibilities" (CF). This therefore connects consequential with deontological thinking at the level of principles.

Table 8.2 Summary of key issues across the doctoral journey

	Probation	Fieldwork and writing-up	Post-viva
Consequential	Anticipated impact on whom? Awareness of consequential ethical thinking Developing reflexivity as a researcher Planning for quality as an ethical issue Who decides what is beneficial?	Avoiding imposition External context to benefit Impact of the study on participants Reviewing aspirations Who decides what is beneficial?	Impact on whom? Local understandings of research Planning for quality Post-study aspirations Reflexivity as a researcher Responsibilities for dissemination Views of reciprocity
Ecological	Cultural appropriateness Researcher positionality Researcher responsibility Role conflict	Awareness of ecological thinking Honesty and openness Micropolitical sensitivity	Academic responsibilities Role conflict Role of gatekeeper
Relational	Awareness of relational ethical thinking Developing contextual understanding Participants' desire to engage	Avoiding imposition Demands on the self Gaining trust Responsibilities to others in the setting	Avoiding imposition Giving people time Not taking sides Putting participants first Reciprocity
Deontological	Duties defined by Western organisations Individual notion of duty Approaches to consent Protecting participants Role ambiguity	Avoiding imposition Guided by participants Protecting participants	Duties defined by Western organisations Honesty and openness Individual notions of duty Putting local values first

From an early stage Alison articulated concerns about the potential for and limitations of what can be anticipated, guiding talk to this issue at several points. An ability to anticipate and be attentive to the "seen, unseen, and unforeseen" (Milner 2007: 388), is partly contingent on prior knowledge.

The post-viva space proved an important opportunity to develop reflexivity as a researcher by revisiting Rafael's earlier consequential concerns that the study would by "ephemeral and any findings might be irrelevant" (CC). Having experienced fieldwork as an ethnographer, he concluded "I think that people can be of value merely for their presence, by taking an interest", thus offering local positive consequences (CL, CN). This reflection extended deliberations about how *reciprocity* might be shown in the field and how ethnography could be a viable and non-threatening research approach. This led Rafael to conclude that an unanticipated benefit of the study was increasing local understandings of research. Rafael felt that although "all teachers are aware about ethnography in the sense of 'a white person going to stay with a tribe and studying the ways of life', there is, to all intents and purposes, no use of ethnography in education research in Ethiopia" (EF). By the end of the study he concluded that staff had a strong sense of what ethnography in education might look like, and it was viewed positively.

One aspect of the UK's Research Excellence Framework (REF) Higher Education Institution assessment process involves assessing a study's reach and significance. The UK Research Excellence Framework terms "reach" and "significance" have particular meanings in evaluating the impact of research. Rafael reflected that dissemination for "reach" was considered the Western norm for doctoral research, and sufficient.

Ecological ethical thinking

Rafael identified the value of ecological ethical thinking in helping a researcher to identify different tiers of actors and expectations in relation to the research site (EC). Accordingly, Rafael specified his value position (Gewirtz & Cribb 2006) as one which sought cultural appropriateness, giving priority to local norms over other principles/rules/laws/agreements including, if necessary, the ethical application to the university (EM).

One issue repeatedly revisited in discussions was the role of a "significant other" in helping Rafael think reflexively. Micheal, with whom Rafael had formerly worked in Ethiopia was a "critical friend, guide by the side" rather than occupying the role of a gatekeeper as presented in research literature; he helped anticipate issues and plan appropriate behaviour throughout the study, as he had done when they were colleagues (EB).

Rafael had considered action-oriented research as a methodological implication of some of the probation phase discussions and also seriously considered entering the field via another VSO placement, but had been told: "You can volunteer with us but you'll have to actually perform a role, you can't just be a researcher!" (EG). After debating potential role conflict as a feature of probationary discussions, Rafael rejected both ideas and clarified his positionality by making a value-led decision on how he wanted to enter the field and be viewed by those in the school setting (EG). He chose an ethnographic study in which he attempted to take on an unobtrusive stance. In doing so, Rafael came to appreciate how ecological thinking was related to "the road not taken" (EC).

Another aspect of Rafael's concerns about role conflict related to anxieties about his academic responsibilities at the university, where he worked as a graduate teaching assistant (EJ). He felt he might be "cheating the university out of its due" (EJ) as a result of his extended periods of fieldwork. In post-viva reflections, he concluded that the clear, firm rules he had expected did not exist and the relationship between his graduate teaching role and the doctoral study was "kind of unofficial" (EJ).

In clarifying multiple constituencies, ecological thinking can prepare a researcher for the challenge that not everyone can be satisfied with the reporting of a study (EQ). To protect oneself against such challenges, the virtuous path of ethical reporting entails being guided by sincerity, rather than concealment or exaggeration, and humility, rather than boastfulness or timidity (Macfarlane 2010).

Relational ethical thinking

Respect is an Aristotelian virtue demonstrated by avoiding partiality (taking sides with one party over another) (Macfarlane 2010). However, this is more straightforward in principle than in practice. Rafael felt that he gained acceptance within the school community by seeking to build trust in his character. This involved giving people time to perceive him as socially acceptable, not taking sides within micropolitical situations, and putting participants first by trying to anticipate whether any specific action was perceived as an imposition. Actions associated with these principles were particularly evident in Rafael's early fieldnotes. "I was worried about not just endangering myself but also others by any kind of reckless behaviour on my part . . . Saying the wrong thing to somebody can easily be done" (RG). This responsibility to others relates to deontological ethics in terms of protecting participants (a "duty of care"), whilst in relational terms it signifies respect and pursuing participants' best interests. In this way the Aristotelian virtue of resoluteness could be an active choice, rather than the vice of laziness or, at the other extreme, a rigid adherence to prepared plans and the vice of inflexibility (Macfarlane 2010).

Rafael was clear from the outset about his desire to "minimise any kind of intrusion into what's going on, bothering people and . . . intervening" (RK). However, a developing contextual understanding led Rafael to appreciate that imposition and avoiding imposition are relative and that imposition is in any case unavoidable, given one's physical presence. He began to judge imposition against how much those in the context appeared to value or show an interest in the study, which related to his search for opportunities for *reciprocity*. For example, he accepted the invitation to award prizes to the eighth-grade students, as refusing to do so would be disrespectful; but he did not deliver on a request for staff training (RK 260218).

Gaining the trust of the majority involved decisions about how to interact with more marginalised community members. Rafael noted with reference to his fieldnotes that "the first kind of key informant I really had in this school was somebody who . . . was undergoing disciplinary procedures for a whole string of alleged offences" (RJ). In the case of this and another staff member, Rafael was guided by tacit micropolitical (ecological) expectations to engage with them cautiously. When one member of staff was rehabilitated, "a couple of months later . . . I felt that it was fine to talk with him, which I did" (EO).

For Rafael, fairness and equity were part of his considerations about how to act relationally, whilst also maximising positive consequences. He concluded that the "potential value is diminished by spreading oneself too thinly . . . The greater scale you work at the less involved with individual teachers and students but the more prestigious and influential the study" (CI 111217). This reflected an ongoing doubt about the study being "ephemeral". However, Rafael argued post-viva that "working at a small scale was a moral decision based on Relational values – eschewing the easier, more prestigious, career-enhancing kinds of research – i.e. people over policy, think global act local etc. etc." (CI).

Deontological ethical thinking

The deontological aspect of ethicality caused considerable challenges in its practical application to this study, especially given its international context. Rafael questioned how to approach this as "I don't think we live in that world anymore where there are kind of fixed views on [deontology]" (DR). Alison explained that she had come to the conclusion that this was a dimension to arrive at after considering the other three dimensions. Rafael challenged this by asking: if "deontology is . . . normative ethics which suggests it is socially influenced, can it be an individual decision based on the balance of evidence as we have been discussing?" (DR 280218). Alison accepted that the framework does indeed prioritise *individual notions of duty* and advocates researcher agency.

It was appreciated that the British Educational Research Association (2011) and Economic Social Research Council (2010/2012) ethical guidelines reflected Western philosophical traditions as well as "the [UK] current political context: compliance, insurance, legalism, neo-liberalism" (DT). This led to a debate about whether or how to apply such guidelines internationally without imposing duties defined by Western organisations. Other texts more fully explore the problematics of using research methods developed in the Global North within the Global South (e.g., Chilisa 2009; Connell 2007; Halai & Wiliam 2011; Hett & Hett 2013; Tikly & Bond 2013).

Rafael noted that the "imperative to put democratic values at the heart of your action [i.e., BERA, 2011] . . . is not consistent with certain non-UK contexts" (DT). A solution was to reject a search for binary (Western/non-Western) thinking (Tikly & Bond 2013) and develop a situated ethical appreciation, such that research is carried out *in* rather than *on* a context (Vithal 2011). This principle matched Rafael's preferred way of researching and saw the continued use of the CERD framework for scaffolding thinking and action.

Rafael wanted to adopt a more democratic approach than the usual application for ministry approval, after which no further discussions of consent would be expected. He felt this would maximise the potential for benefitting, rather than imposing on, participants (EA). From early in the study he sought opportunities to learn from other researchers' experiences in the context, taking guidance in particular from the Young Lives project (Morrow 2013), which advised about the inappropriateness of standard UK approaches to gaining signed, informed consent, in favour of regularly checking consent verbally and not requesting signatures (EG).

The ERB considered Rafael's proposal favourably. The enabling characteristics of the ERB in this particular university were concluded to be: a) opportunities for discussion with the board to make further justifications or consider different options; b) the inclusion of supervisors in the same field on the board; and c) the cross-disciplinary nature of the board; all points supported by Israel (2015).

In the field, whilst Rafael was guided by his obligations to the ERB, his stance was to "put local values first" (DS). Not to do so would, he concluded, have bound him to foreign/external standards of conduct – a form of cultural imperialism (DS 04032018). This saw him adapting his schedule according to invitations in the field (DU). He concluded that his notion of duty prioritised patience, listening, showing empathy and compromise (at least in terms of time), underpinned by a desire to build relationships. Rafael prioritised relational (contextualised) over deontological (normative principled) thinking to create *individual notions of duty*. Whilst the outcome might be particular to Rafael, engagement with the CERD framework supported him in articulating and justifying this approach.

Conclusion

This concrete example of a doctoral journey allows more general discussion about reflection in, on, about and for research through an operationalisation of "ethical reflexivity" (Gewirtz & Cribb 2006; Abraham 2008; Hammersley 2008). The empirical study presented examined the sustained and mutual ethical exploration of issues associated with, first, the doctoral researcher's positionality in relation to the research site; second, the non-Western setting for the study; and third, the ethnographic methodology adopted. Whilst dialogic approaches have been presented for use in scaffolding ethical appraisal (e.g., Mustajoki & Mustajoki 2017), this chapter contributes to a gap in the literature about the value, conceptualisation and operationalisation of such approaches within doctoral supervisory relationships.

In common with most studies, not only doctoral, some of the issues that were identified, examined and resolved could be anticipated, while others arose as the study progressed. Through the systematic analysis of dialogue in spaces created to support ethical decision-making, this chapter evidences that the CERD ethical appraisal framework can be used iteratively to apply four ethical lenses through the duration of a study. The consequential and deontological dimensions help researchers to reify principles to which they are committed; the ecological and relational dimensions provide opportunities to reflect on how these may apply in the particular context of study, and to clarify the researcher's positionality in relation to different constituencies within and beyond the study site. Instead of relying on actions based on normative principles alone, which have been shown, when problematised, to be limited and reductive, researchers can be supported to make decisions and evaluate their actions in situ. This also ensures that a strong connection is made between methodological and ethical issues of quality. Such ethical work supports preparation for ERBs, fieldwork, reporting and dissemination. Explicit ethical reflexivity enables ethical learning to be made visible as changes in thinking, decision-making and action. This articulation is supported by current debates related to ethical reflexivity as recommended to researchers, whether working alone or in teams.

In particular, this study demonstrates how the repeated application of the framework helps exceed professional socialisation, if defined as "adopt[ing] the values, skills, attitudes, norms and knowledge needed for membership in a given society, group or organisation" (Golde 1998, cited in Mawson & Abbott 2017), by engaging with other researchers in discursive spaces. This could be as true for any researcher working in a team or collaborative setting as it was for Rafael as a doctoral researcher. It has been shown how it is possible for researchers (even those with differential status) to challenge and extend the values, skills and attitudes of both researchers involved in the ethical discussions, rather than a researcher simply adopting those of others. Rather than merely accessing a research culture (Deem & Brehony 2000), researchers can contribute to it. This has been illustrated by Rafael as an early career researcher developing independence in thinking, in terms of ethicality.

An issue not anticipated in the original presentation of the framework (Stutchbury & Fox 2009) is the value of engaging with the four dimensions in a particular order – giving rise to the CERD acronym. There is particular value in starting and ending with consequential thinking, which helps to clarify to whom and how benefits might be maximised. Rafael found it insufficient to limit consideration of these issues to the planning stages of research, as the significance of such practical commitments are not necessarily apparent until the closing stages of thesis writing. Further, Rafael identifies enacting beneficence as an aspect of doctoral (specifically PhD) study not emphasised in local academic culture or doctoral assessment criteria. He, like other researchers such as Gewirtz and Cribb (2006), argues enacting beneficence should be.

The mutuality of learning which is possible between researchers has also been evidenced; in this case, between doctoral researcher and supervisor (Halse 2011). This was shown by how the framework itself was developed conceptually, as well as its application to a particular study. Through working with Rafael, Alison learnt about the suitability of the framework in an international context with which she was unfamiliar. Rafael learnt how the framework might support comprehensive ethical analysis, and the development of an academically defensible case for undertaking the kind of research which he thought would be useful in the Ethiopian setting. Recognising the situated knowledge Rafael brought, Alison took the role of a peer in discussions of culturally appropriate ways of studying in Tigray, whilst she brought into the spaces for discussion the framework as a tool to facilitate discussion and decision-making.

A key contribution of this chapter has been to propose a set of spaces in which to operationalise Gewirtz and Cribb's (2006) recommendations for ethical reflexivity, with the CERD framework offering a deliberative rather than prescriptive approach to supporting ethical appraisal.

First, the scaffolded spaces enabled digging under the surface to "be explicit, as far as is possible, about the value assumptions and evaluative judgements that inform or are embedded in every stage of [the] research" (Gewirtz & Cribb 2006: 147). The application of the CERD framework in spaces of mutual ethical exploration therefore makes a methodological contribution to revealing hidden agendas and tensions. Whilst there is evidence that this was possible in relation to the focus of the doctoral study, ethical issues related to the wider supervisory relationship (which impacted on the doctoral journey) had been inadvertently hidden (Deuchar 2008; Halse 2011; Watts 2010). These included anxieties about the doctoral researchers' academic responsibilities and the impact of the supervisor's multiple roles. This challenges how fully self-reflexive both researchers were able to be during their formal engagement with one another. The implications of this are that a supervisor's application of the framework needs to be as open to self-reflexivity as that of the doctoral researcher, something that Alison was not able to fully achieve until the conclusion of the doctoral study. The spaces need to be safe enough and the relationship strong enough that such agendas and tensions can be voiced. In the case of this study, the power relationship of the supervisor to doctoral researcher roles pre-viva appears to have silenced Rafael's willingness to articulate certain concerns. How this imbalance can be overcome is something for further work within such spaces. This need for safety, honesty and equality will also apply to research teams in which there are power differentials if individual values are to be revealed, challenged and applied to the project in question.

Related to this, second, the spaces showed both researchers were "prepared to offer a defence of [their] assumptions and judgements [to] the extent that either they might not be shared by others or, conversely, that they are not sufficiently problematised by others" (Gewirtz & Cribb 2006: 147). This saw Alison shifting from initiating discussions by airing reflections on her own research (opening them up to challenge), to inviting Rafael to reflect on and present rationales for his own decisions. These justifications needed to be open to the inevitable problematisation and critique by supervisors, the ERB, the *viva voce* committee and, as Rafael notes, also when publishing. The requirement to defending one's work is not unique to doctoral research, and is expected of all those presenting their work to the academic community. It has been shown how the CERD framework can be used to identify how a study might satisfy multiple audiences.

Third, the use of the CERD framework to support dialogue has been shown to be useful in "acknowledging, and where possible responding to, tensions between the various values that are embedded in our research" (Gewirtz & Cribb 2006: 147). The dimensions of the framework, drawn from four traditions of ethical thinking (Flinders 1992), offer alternative lenses through which to identify, examine and resolve issues and tensions.

Finally, using the CERD framework as a deliberative rather than prescriptive tool opened it up to further development and allowed insightful discussions about the appropriateness of applying the framework to a non-Western – in this case, Tigrayan – school setting. This allowed both researchers to "take seriously the practical judgements and dilemmas of the people we are researching" (Gewirtz & Cribb 2006: 148). Drawing on his own experiences, a review of methodological and substantive literature and his relationships with Micheal, others in the school community and a growing network of researchers working in the Global South, Rafael became increasingly aware of local practical considerations. Some issues he was able to anticipate, and others had to be addressed when encountered in the field. This chapter adds to others in this book in showing how ethical reflexivity needs to support culturally appropriate, situated ethical ethnographic study.

Implications for theory building about ethical reflexivity in doctoral study

Using the CERD framework as part of doctoral supervision allows a response to Gewirtz and Cribb's (2006) three key challenges to ethical reflexivity and leads towards a set of recommendations. First, they note the need to deal with the apparent boundlessness of ethical reflexivity. Rafael noted this as a challenge for doctoral studies, stimulated by Alison repeatedly raising the agenda of impact in terms of reach and significance when reviewing how positive consequences might be maximised for multiple audiences. In terms of obligations, Rafael was clear that he had satisfied the university ERB, his doctoral examiners and continues to satisfy academic journal editors on ethical grounds as he publishes from his thesis. However, as a result of ethical reflections, he is now not fully satisfied in terms of dissemination to the local context itself. Such dissatisfactions can be a powerful driver for further research (and development) work, motivating researchers to make a difference with their research. Rafael is now a postdoctoral researcher focusing on education in Africa, and is in a position to build on and share his knowledge of culturally sensitive practice in such settings. Ethical learning as an ongoing process can fuel further study and possible future benefits.

Second, Gewirtz and Cribb (2006) noted the challenge of handling the resolution of abstract dilemmas with practical solutions. Rafael's emergent principle of observing the "status quo" and putting "local values first" foregrounded his practical decision-making and also shaped both researchers' joint understanding of what cultural appropriateness might look like as ethical practice. This involved an ethical education for Alison, as supervisor, as it did for the ERB, as to what was reasonable to expect in terms of adapting UK/Western norms to a Tigrayan setting. Review boards need to be open to such reflexivity (Israel 2015). This raises the question about how the outcomes of ethical reflexivity born out of fieldwork can be cascaded for the benefit of future researchers. Are there spaces in our institutions for ERBs to learn about the realities of culturally appropriate fieldwork beyond the early engagement they have with researchers in authorising data collection?

Gewirtz and Cribb's final challenge to ethical reflexivity relates to "balancing ethicality and methodological rigour when reporting" (2006: 148). Building on the point above, such decision-making supports the need for ongoing discussions about the ethicality of a study at all stages of its progression. Unanticipated ethical issues can arise when reporting, as well as during fieldwork. What part can our ERBs play in supporting researchers? There is talk in the UK of ERBs playing a monitoring role in studies (BERA 2018). If this involves touching base and supporting decision-making for issues which have arisen post-approval, this will be a new and useful space for ethical reflexivity. However, if this becomes a prescriptive monitoring process checking that studies have been carried out as previously planned and/or threatening to derail studies which have deviated from this plan, then an opportunity for ethical reflexivity and learning will be missed.

Note

1 Flinders' (1992) analysis of four ethical traditions, which informed the Stutchbury and Fox ethical appraisal framework, is presented as Table 1.3 in Chapter 1.

References

British Educational Research Association (BERA). 2011. "BERA Ethical Guidelines for Educational Research". London: BERA. www.bera.ac.uk/wp-content/uploads/2014/02/BERA-Ethical-Guidelines-2011.pdf.

British Educational Research Association (BERA). 2018. "BERA Ethical Guidelines for Educational Research", 4th edn. London: BERA. www.bera.ac.uk/wp-content/uploads/2018/06/BERA-Ethical-Guidelines-for-Educational-Research_4thEdn_2018.pdf?noredirect=1.

Carpenter, D. 2013. "Generic Ethics Principles in Social Science Research Discussion 'Stimulus' Paper for Symposium 1". In Generic Ethics Principles in Social Science Research, Professional Briefings 3, 3–6. London: Academy of Social Sciences.

Chang, H. 2016. Autoethnography as Method. London: Routledge.

Chilisa, B. 2009. "Indigenous African-centred ethics". In The Handbook of Social Research Ethics, edited by D. Mertens and P. Ginsberg, 407–425. Thousand Oaks, CA: Sage.

Connell, R. 2007. Southern Theory: The Global Dynamics of Knowledge in Social Science. Cambridge: Polity.

Deem, R. and Brehony, K.J. 2000. "Doctoral researchers' access to research cultures – are some more unequal than others?" Studies in Higher Education 25(2): 149–165.

Deuchar, R. 2008. "Facilitator, director or critical friend?: Contradiction and congruence in doctoral supervision styles". Teaching in Higher Education 13(4): 489–500.

Driver, J. 2011. Consequentialism. London: Routledge.

Flinders, D. 1992. "In search of ethical guidance: Constructing a basis for dialogue". Qualitative Studies in Education 5(2): 101–115.

Gewirtz, S. and Cribb, A. 2006. "What to do about values in social research: The case for ethical reflexivity in the sociology of education?" British Journal of Sociology of Education 27(2): 141–155.

Gilligan, C. 2011. *Joining the Resistance*. New York: Polity Press.

Golde, C.M. 1998. "Beginning graduate school: Explaining first year doctoral attrition". *New Directions for Higher Education* 101(1): 55–64.

Halai, A. and Wiliam, D., eds. 2011. *Research Methodologies in the 'South'*. Karachi, PA: Oxford University Press.

Halse, C. 2011 "'Becoming a supervisor': The impact of doctoral supervision on supervisors' learning". *Studies in Higher Education* 36(5): 557–570.

Hett, G. and Hett, J. 2013. "Ethics in intercultural research: Reflections on the challenges of conducting field research in a Syrian context". *Compare: A Journal of Comparative and International Education* 43(4): 496–515.

Israel, M. 2015. *Research Ethics and Integrity for Social Scientists*. Los Angeles, CA: Sage.

Macfarlane, B. 2010. "Values and virtues in qualitative research". In *New Approaches to Qualitative Research: Wisdom and Uncertainty*, edited by M. Savin-Baden and C.H. Major, 19–27. New York: Routledge.

Mawson, K. and Abbott, I. 2017. "Supervising the professional doctoral researcher: Less process and progress, more peripheral participation and personal identity". *Management in Education* 31(4): 187–193.

Milligan, L. 2016. "Insider-outsider-inbetweener? Researcher positioning, participative methods and cross-cultural educational research". *Compare: A Journal of Comparative and International Education* 46(2): 235–250.

Milner, H.R. 2007. "Race, culture, and researcher positionality: Working through dangers seen, unseen, and unforeseen". *Educational Researcher* 36(7): 388–400.

Mitchell, R. 2017a. "An ethnographic case study of the agendas, participation and influence of stakeholders at an urban government primary school in Tigray, Ethiopia". PhD dissertation, University of Leicester.

Mitchell, R. 2017b. "Democracy or control? The participation of management, teachers, students and parents in school leadership in Tigray, Ethiopia". *International Journal of Educational Development* 55(1): 49–55.

Mitchell, R. 2017c. "Radical student participation: Lessons from an urban government primary school in Tigray, Ethiopia". *Compare: A Journal of Comparative and International Education*. Doi: 10.1080/03057925.2017.1385390.

Morrow, V. 2013. "Practical ethics in social research with children and families in young lives: A longitudinal study of childhood poverty in Ethiopia, Andhra Pradesh (India), Peru and Vietnam". *Methodological Innovations Online* 8(1): 21–35.

Mustajoki, M. and Mustajoki, A. 2017. *A New Approach to Research Ethics: Using Guided Dialogue to Strengthen Research Communities*. London: Routledge.

Noddings, N. 1984. *Caring: A Feminine Approach to Ethics and Moral Education*. Berkeley, CA: University of California Press.

Reynolds, P.D. 1979. *Ethical Dilemmas and Social Science Research: An Analysis of Moral Issues Confronting Investigators in Research Using Human Participants*. San Francisco, CA: Jossey-Bass.

Rossman, G.B. and Rallis, S.F. 2010. "Everyday ethics: Reflections on practice". *International Journal of Qualitative Studies in Education* 23(4): 379–391.

Scheffler, S., ed. 1988. *Consequentialism and Its Critics*. Oxford: Oxford University Press.

Seedhouse, D. 1998. *Ethics: The Heart of Healthcare*. Chichester: Wiley

Stutchbury, K. and Fox, A. 2009. "Ethics in educational research: Introducing a methodological tool for effective ethical analysis". *Cambridge Journal of Education* 39(4): 489–504.

Tikly, L. and Bond, T. 2013. "Towards a post-colonial research ethics in comparative and international education". *Compare: A Journal of Comparative and International Education* 43(4): 422–442.

Vithal, R. 2011. "Research, researchers and researching in the South". In *Research Methodologies in the 'South'*, edited by A. Halai and D. Wiliam, 18–32. Karachi, PA: Oxford University Press.

Wallace, M. and Poulson, L. 2003. *Learning to Read Critically in Educational Leadership and Management*. London: Sage.

Watts, J.H. 2010. "Team supervision of the doctorate: Managing roles, relationships and contradictions". *Teaching in Higher Education* 15(3): 335–339.

Part IV

Interconnecting webs

Chapter 9

Emergent issues in ethnographic ethics

Futures and possibilities

Barbara Dennis

Introduction

The authors whose works are included in this book bring to light the most contemporary debates on ethics in ethnographic practices. Research ethics are not
resolved at the point of ethical review board approval and, as is argued quite
consistently throughout the book, neither are review board approval policies and
mandates capable of entirely guiding the ethical practices of ethnographers. In
this concluding chapter of the book, I reframe the insights across the chapters
through a dialogic conceptualisation of ethics. In so doing, I foreground what
seem to be key emergent issues in educational ethnographic ethics. I conclude
the chapter with ideas about futures and possibilities for educational ethnographers. Ethnography is a particularly engaged form of social science research that
emphasises long-term participatory involvement in the field of study over time.
The participatory aspects require researchers to participate in the practices, rituals
and meaning-making of the field site in ways that take up participant perspectives.
Simultaneously, ethnography also requires its participants to engage with the
research in ways that allow the research(er) into their spaces and practices. This
kind of rich participatory engagement is not essentially procedural in nature as it
is interpersonal in the first place: relational, contextual and particular. Chapters
in this volume lodge important and serious critiques of the work of institutional
review boards both in terms of the insufficiency of formal proceduralism in ethical accountability for ethnography and in terms of the potential damage such
formalism can sustain if it is not mediated. Future possibilities point towards
what exceeds the contemporary bureaucracies of review boards. The complexities of the field must be ethically navigated and these complexities account for
more of the ethical labor in ethnography. There are three sections to this
chapter: (a) a dialogic reframing of ethics; (b) emergent insights and issues for
ethnographic ethics; and (c) futures and possibilities.

A dialogic reframing of ethics

To begin, I want to set forth a dialogic description of ethics. Across the chapters
in this book, such a way of thinking about ethics is both explicit (for example,

Fox and Mitchell, Chapter 8, this volume) and implicit (for example, Beach & Arrazola, Chapter 3, this volume). A dialogic understanding of ethics helps us locate its intersubjective quality, its situatedness, its fallibility and its deliberative nature. Global conversations about the role of review boards on the one hand and increasing (see Chapter 3, this volume) inclusion of participants and communities to which we might hold ourselves accountable (Busher, Chapter 5, this volume; Lather 2009), on the other hand, suggest that our ethical work will become more than ours alone (Dennis 2018). Dialogue about ethics promises to push our thinking about ethics and our capacities to engage ethically through ethnography towards what is better without assuming that one is better is universal or fixed. Busher and Fox (Chapter 1, this volume) introduce us to a framework for thinking about ethics (Kitchener & Kitchener 2009) that lends itself nicely to introducing the dialogic quality of ethics.

When we reframe our conversation about ethics through dialogue, it is easier to see that ethics are not only contextualised, but their engagement will also involve a form of deliberation that is not fixed. Ethical principles (such as might be articulated in a professional code of practice) might reach toward expanding universals (which we could roughly define as reaching towards an increasingly inclusive agreement). Nevertheless, application of those principles will involve local contextual instantiations and should never be straight-forwardly accepted without at least an implicit dialogic interpretation, translation or transformation (see Beach & Arrazola, Chapter 3, this volume). "Education ethnographers place themselves in the practical domain of everyday life where the course of one's ethical actions is much more interdependently and situationally forged not prior to the conduct of research, but as part of the process itself" (Dennis 2010: 123). The tension between the formalised proceduralism that accompanies our institutional leash as scholars and our on-the-ground interpersonal, interdependent relationships in the field becomes part of an ongoing dialogue that must remain open and engaged (see Nikkanen, Chapter 6, and Traianou, Chapter 2, this volume). The either/or framing can then be decentered through the particular contexts within which ethnographers are working out the ethical aspects of their research endeavours. What each of the authors in this text insightfully suggests is that there should be no uncritical (or fundamentalist) uptake of either ethical procedures or ethical standards. Fox and Mitchell (Chapter 8) deliver this point explicitly as they share the intimacy of their own dialogue. A dialogic orientation releases us from expecting the conversations across the two spheres to be one. We do not have to reduce one to the other (Smette, Chapter 4). Neither do we have to strictly apply the content of one conversation to the practices of the other conversation (Traianou, Chapter 2; Beach & Arrazola, Chapter 3).

Figure 9.1 illustrates the structural and character differences, dialogically speaking, between review boards, ethnographic fields and the spaces between. Dialogue with/in the sphere of review boards positions the researcher as "less-expert", "needy", and "technocratic". Dialogue with/in the sphere of the ethnographic field positions the researcher as "fallible", "responsible" and

Table 9.1 Ethical decision-making as dialogue

Kitchner and Kitchner (2009) levels of ethical decision-making	Explicit dialogue as ethics	Implicit dialogue as ethics	References to these dialogues in the text (chapter authors)
1 Researcher decision-making in their own research setting	Dialogue of ethical practices informed by local culture and relationships; dialogues of access	Refraining from accepting at face value the practices of a community as ethical – a willingness to acknowledge the ethical fallibility of local practices; dialogues of inclusion; dialogues of belonging; dialogues of self-awareness	Smette (Chapter 4) Nikkanen (Chapter 6) Dovemark (Chapter 7) Fox and Mitchell (Chapter 8)
2 Professional codes of ethics	Legal dialogue	Negotiating and/or recognising of the spirit of the codes in practice as it contrasts with the literal articulation of the code; dialogues of self-commitment	Smette (Chapter 4) Traianou (Chapter 2) Beach and Arrazola (Chapter 3) Nikkanen (Chapter 6)
3 Ethical principles	Philosophical and moral dialogue underlying the legal and codified dialogue of Level 2	Deliberating the complexities of harm and vulnerability; recognising power and working to instantiate equity and transformation as characteristics of the dialogues	Traianou (Chapter 2) Busher (Chapter 5)
4 Higher-level deliberation on ethical principles	Self (which is intimately practical) in relation to philosophical and moral dialogue	Democratising the research process in ways that allow the self to become wounded (McLaren)	Fox and Mitchell (Chapter 8) Dovemark (Chapter 7) Busher (Chapter 5) Nikkanen (Chapter 6)
5 Meta-ethical decision-making	Dialogue about ethics (such as what this book does overall)	Deliberations about ethics that change how we understand our own ethical commitments; confronting disjunctures between the talk about ethics and ethical doings we explicate through reflection	Fox and Mitchell (Chapter 8) Beach and Arrazola (Chapter 3) Busher (Chapter 5)

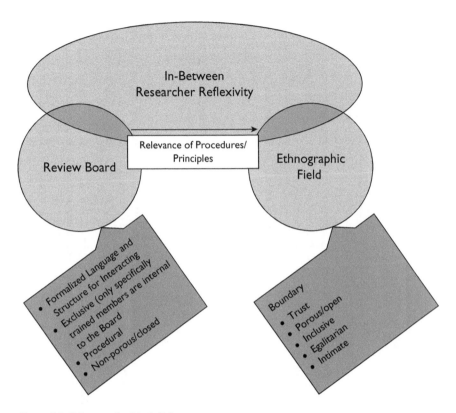

Figure 9.1 Spheres of ethical dialogue

"committed". The researcher herself finds a reflective, engaged, uncertain, inchoate subject in the flow of acting in-between.

Each sphere manifests different kinds of dialogic opportunities/constraints positioning the ethnographer as an interlocutor in an already ongoing conversation. Each sphere is bounded. The space between makes it possible for the researcher to reflect, transform and continue on. There is a formal link between the review board and the ethnographic field which has to do with categories of formal action such as gaining access and gaining informed consent, but this link is mediated by the person of the researcher herself.

Dialogue with/in the sphere of review boards

Researchers are positioned in a formal dialogue with review boards as that which needs to be governed, managed, sanctioned, approved and legitimised. Such dialogue is required even if the point of the conversation is to have a review board validate an exemption of its own approval for any particular study in question.

In fact, the conversation with review board members happens primarily on paper through highly regulated language and structure. Within review boards, trained academics and staff deliberate on proposed research studies with the authority to restrict, cancel or deny the right to conduct the study on supposedly ethical grounds. The process is largely technocratised and bureaucratised, which means that the communication is primarily truncated, controlled and minimal. Researchers know not to say too much. Deliberations are reserved for members of a review board. As pointed out by Beach and Arrazola in this text (Chapter 3), review boards tend to masquerade legalistic anxieties as an imperative to protect human subjects through control of research practices.

The boundaries around the review board sphere are relatively fixed, exclusive, highly structured and formal, resulting in highly controlled, formally written requests from researchers for legitimate approval. Neither the dialogue nor the fruits of that dialogue can escape these limitations. Ethnographers must engage with this sphere through strategic action, for example, using specific procedures to gather informed consent, even when one's own ethical frameworks require an ongoing orientation towards consent. Thus, proceduralism marks both the means and the ends of communicative intent and possibility between researchers obtaining review board approvals/exemptions. The chapters in this text have clarified the ways in which this proceduralism is detrimental, limiting and insufficient for ethical guidance. Such truncated dialogues can only secure ethical confidence through outcomes and procedures. The entire ethical "conversation" between researchers and their corresponding review boards functions through this proceduralism. However, within the review board sphere, members might revise procedures, determine fit and examine breaches and complaints through dialogue.

There are pressures in the production of these boundaries – some of those pressures come from global movements, professional organisations and monitoring bodies. The boundaries are part of a closed bureaucratic management system in place to regulate research activities over which there is little meaningful control. Perhaps also significant is the content (not just procedures) through which the deliberations occur – the content is equally limiting. For example, review board "conversations" with researchers might focus on a highly operationalised and technocratised form of consent universalising the concept of consent across all forms of inquiry.

Dialogue with/in the sphere of the ethnographic field

The ethnographic field is diverse and complex. As Smette reminds us (Chapter 4), our field ethics cannot be reduced to formalised procedures. Researchers enter its porous borders. Those borders are constituted of some shared linguistic and cultural knowledge. Interactions across and within those borders are ongoing, open, situated and complicated. Ethnographers actually interact with those in the sphere. Ethics are not superimposed from the outside, but instead are anchored at least partially in the community itself. Review board regulations and procedures are strategically followed though disconnected from the kinds of ethical conversations and experiences ethnographers encounter in their fieldwork.

As researchers engage with participants in the field, they encounter not only their own commitments and values, but contradictory and complicated values and commitments held by their participants. The relationalities are lively (Barad 2008) and rife with potentiality. Each encounter, and the site as a whole, provides ethnographers with varied moments to foreground the ethical nature of their work. The kinds of dialogues that emerge might be dialogues around dilemmas, disagreements, fostering social justice and equity, critiquing cultural practices of harm or examining together systemic inequalities and oppressions. Such conversations, both explicit and implicit, can fuel ethical decision-making, intimacy, critique and transformation. These conversations are best when characterised by openness, inclusivity, an articulation of values and freedom from the effects of both power and fear (drawing on Habermas 1998). These dialogues typically match the preferences of participants and use a less-formalised vocabulary and structure when compared with that of review boards.

The demands of field-based ethical dialogues are both personal and political. The resolution of ethical dilemmas (even the recognition of a situation as an ethical dilemma) is one that necessarily involves the self, one's identity in relation with others (including non-human others). These conversations offer clear opportunities for negotiations which sometimes include participants. One cannot anticipate from the outset what these dilemmas will be, nor how they should be resolved. Moreover, the formal "conversation" with the review board committee does not have much to offer this conversation. Though there might be some shared values – for example, doing no harm – such shared values are insufficient in and of themselves to resolve ethical dilemmas. Moreover, the community can never be thought of as a monolith and researchers will not have equally good relationships across participants. As Dovemark (Chapter 7) reported, sometimes our participants get angry with us and we are left to figure out how to move forward ethically without abusing power or privileging our own perspectives. We must mindfully harness opportunities for ethical dialogue drawing more on *phrónēsis* (both skill and an orientation toward the good, as explained in Chapter 2, this volume) than proceduralism. What surfaces ethically is not simply a matter of a researcher choosing one particular act or another based on the ethical situation and context, but a dialogue of possibilities. Other people at the site will also be involved and implicated (Dennis 2018).

Ethical dialogues in this sphere are not pinned to strategic action and can include the possibility for transformation. These dialogues may be primed through review board constructs such as "vulnerability" fostering a particular way of thinking about participants. Nevertheless, engagements with participants may belie the label "vulnerable" and push us toward a concept of empowerment and liberation (see Chapter 5, this volume). Our understanding of vulnerability, for example, seeps outside any formal review board structure to include, also, an explicit conversation about how to have an ethical conversation on vulnerability.

Dialogue with/in the between sphere of the ethnographic field and the review board

Authors of this book wrote timely chapters largely focused on the dialogue of ethics within the ethnographic field. The link between the regulatory mandates of review boards and the ethical field practices of ethnographers was critiqued. By reframing ethics as dialogue, it becomes clear that the conversational structures, boundaries, potentials and limitations are in many ways not compatible.

The between sphere is inhabited by researchers who must locate themselves ethically as people (Dennis 2018), be responsive to the two spheres (more if we add in the professional sphere of ethics detailed in by Nikkanen in Chapter 6 of this volume or other institutional and communal domains) and find ways to stretch themselves like bridges between the two spheres. Unlike the other two spheres, this one is a metaphorical and reflective. When one can unproblematically move between the two spheres, one might just experience the two dialogic orientations as different without feeling troubled by those differences. Unfortunately, many education ethnographers describe the incompatibility of the two or the insufficiency of one in relation with the other. Additionally, our own personal ethics or sense of ourselves as moral agents can be odds with the directives of a review board or the ongoing practices of our field site. Dovemark in this volume (Chapter 7) tells the powerful story of having to face her own critical aims for research in the face of significant anger and personal derogation from her participants. She had to step outside of the immediacy of the field to reflect and recompose her sense of self/identity within the demands

Table 9.2 Comparison of spheres of researcher dialogic engagement

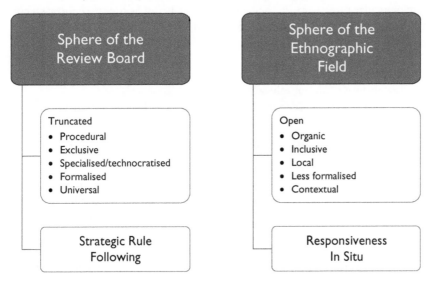

of the field. Nikkanen easily identified with practitioners in the field, but found herself at odds with the review board regulations. This in-between "space" is an opportunity to reflect on ethical decisions and engagements by identifying one's self in both spheres and in terms of both one's own ethical desires for one's self and one's skill (*phrónēsis*, as we are introduced to it by Traianou in Chapter 2 of this volume). The reflection can manifest as a dialogue with a particular other, as we see illustrated by Fox and Mitchell (see Chapter 8, this volume). In this reflection, academic and ordinary structures can guide the dialogue. If we look closely at the conversation between Fox and Mitchell, we see that the reflection as a deliberative process fostered by the freedom to be honest and authentic without punishment, care and the operationalisation of ethical appraisals.

This betweenness provides a scholar with opportunities to meet praxis needs as an ethical researcher – to see herself through the moral and ethical complexity of fieldwork. One is also able to engage in meta-dialogue about ethical dialogues. The present text is a great example of such a dialogue. Not all authors in the book agree with one another and, yet, each contributes to fostering a thoughtful engagement with the possibilities of behaving ethically as an ethnographer. This between space is both personal and political, but at the end of the day demands that a researcher take responsibility for their own ethical decision-making for one's self.

Emergent insights and issues for ethnographic ethics

In this section of the paper, I highlight three emergent insights/issues for ethnographic ethics. By foregrounding the dialogic nature of ethics, it is possible to draw out several patterns of insight and issues. I have chosen to focus on these particular three because they indicate what I read as the three most salient patterns of concern across the chapters in this book. These insights/issues are organised according to three large questions.

1   How relevant are review board procedures for ethnographic practice?
2   How inclusive can our ethical practices be?
3   How can our ethical accountability foster social and personal transformation?

How relevant are review board procedures for ethnographic practice?

One key point across these chapters is that distinctly different modes and structures of ethical dialogue are at play in research efforts which problematise the value of review boards for guiding ethical practices for ethnographers. The distinction between the procedural application of overarching principles and the ongoing negotiation of ethics with participants was a persistent theme in the book; however, through our dialogic reformulation, we can imagine that these distinct conversations do not put each other at risk. Both spheres of dialogue can find a parallel coexistence without subverting the field negotiations to the procedural conversation. The procedural conversation is a truncated and limited one, not capable of adjudicating or deliberating on the more detailed and rich ethical conversation of the field, but researchers are left wondering how relevant the two conversations are for one another.

How relevant are the review board imperatives for ethnographers? When scholars find the procedures difficult, superfluous or damaging, they may engage with those procedures only because they are required to do so. When scholars are relieved that their studies are labelled exempt, it seems that researchers are not really find much value in the going through the process for their own ethical practices. In other words, ethnographic researchers end up interacting with review boards only to satisfy strategic, institutional goals which are not coherently linked to their ethnographic fieldwork. When the "review board sphere" (Figure 9.1; Table 9.2) of ethics becomes untethered from ethical practices in the field, then those ethics lose their reflective advantage for researchers and institutions fail to adequately support scholars in their research endeavours. On the other hand, there is no desirable way for an institutional review board to be actively engaged in the related field site sphere of ethical decision-making. Researchers would be discouraged from providing too much information from the site and from using the language and concerns of the site to complete the formal paperwork. The dialogue of the field site sphere only seems to become relevant for the review board at the beginning/end and only then again if a complaint is filed. Yet, disengagement from the field site renders both their ethical management of ethnography and their legal self-protection somewhat ineffective.

The distinction between these two conversations produces a pressure for the ethnographer in-between. Ethnographic participants rarely even recognise their rather minimal actual role in the dialogue of the "review board sphere". However, researchers can keenly feel the pressures associated with the disjuncture between these two conversations. Thus, the question is how does an ethnographer productively engage with both conversations – productively for their own practices and their own sense of self? A related issue, then, has to do with the variably positioned ethnographer in the two conversations. What is the ethnographer's presumed ethical expertise across these two conversations? How is that expertise practised in ways that reduce the felt pressure of the disjuncture?

How inclusive can our ethical practices be?

Both the Busher (Chapter 5) and Beach and Arrazola (Chapter 3) chapters in this volume raise the issue of ethical inclusion. Busher raises this question in the context of deeply including participants themselves in research. He argues that meaningfully including participants in the research process is a way to strengthen our ethical decision-making in the field. His chapter causes us to relocate the question of ethics from a realm external to the participants themselves towards a conversation internal to the participants and inclusive of their perspectives. Any ethical deliberations that can happen without meaningful engagement with participants would not be inclusive enough. Dovemark's chapter, on the other hand, begins with an ethical call-out by one set of participants – basically calling her a liar. In this case, the ethical dialogue also falls short because the claims made by this particular group of participants does not include those for whom the claims have ramifications – not just Dovemark, but also students whose lives are significantly negatively affected by the attitudes reflected in the rejection of Dovemark's findings as lies.

What does it mean to be inclusive when there are ethical disagreements? First of all, equalising power relations so that participants can speak into the process – this is a fundamental layer of inclusion. This does not imply that participant perspectives themselves will reflect a higher or more acceptable level of ethics, but just that their perspectives ought to be part of the deliberations. Ethical deliberations and the outcomes of those deliberations owe their accountability to all who would be affected by the deliberations themselves (Dennis 2018). There are practical, interpersonal and ideological challenges to this kind of inclusion, though it remains a worthwhile question: how inclusive can our ethical practices be? It takes some skill to engage in ethical deliberations – how can we work with our participants to develop such conversations so that, at the end of the day, they are not stunting the conversations with the kinds of dialogue-stopping proclamations made by Dovemark's participants?

Beach and Arrazola argue that review boards are not fully inclusive in their ethical purview. For example, they raise concern for the geopolitical world and other non-human material relevant to ethnographic research practices. Review boards focus on human subjects, but this limited view of ethics results in ignoring ethical responsibilities to care for earth and other materiality of the society. This critique points out a limitation regarding the ethical conversation of the "review board sphere". Review boards are, also, not inclusive in process. For example, one must be specially trained to be included in the conversation board members have as it uses highly specified language and skill. Interactions with the board are heavily regulated, even down to the format one must use to submit for approval. Review boards issue approvals that are required for publication, receipt of grant funding and so on. Further, the conversation with the board is not optional – institutionally affiliated researchers in many European and North American countries are required to obtain approval or exemption from the board for each and every study. In Dovemark's example, review boards could have better taken into account the larger questions of social oppression in their concern for human subjects – thinking beyond the subjects who might be participating in the ethnographic study. The question becomes: are there ways that review boards could be more inclusive without wading too far into the field dialogue where the structures should not be so formalised or technically managed?

How can our ethical accountability foster social and personal transformation?

Beach and Arrazola specifically lament the failure of review boards to contribute actively to the transformation of an oppressive social world. Dovemark took this problem on herself, thinking of the much-needed social change in school access and school choice; Dovemark at last claimed accountability to her own personal commitments for social justice transformation. As an ongoing dialogue, our ethical decision-making can be linked to both our own transformation as people and the transformation of others. Beach and Arrazola implicitly distinguish between a legal dialogue and a justice dialogue – specifically locating the aims of education in part with a justice dialogue. The authors point out that review boards (in part because the bureaucratic and technocratic procedures mask the legal anxieties) produce ethical failures and perhaps among those would be implicit resistance to social transformation.

Transformative doings for the good, for justice (including geological justice) benefit from the kinds of conversations that are more open, inclusive and egalitarian (see Busher, Chapter 5, and Fox & Mitchell, Chapter 8, this volume). Power relations will put such characteristics at risk (Habermas 1998). If the truncated, closed technocratic conversation with review boards is given power over the field then such risks are enfolded into the research process and transformative goals can be lost. In my agreement with my university's review board I had agreed that I would minimise the harm for participants – and all participants were considered equal. Yet, throughout the life of the ethnography it became clear that in the field there were bullies. Our team research efforts had an opportunity to transform the bullying practices of the school, but only if we were willing to let the research uncover specific identities those doing the bullying (some of them teachers). Now the ethical dilemma becomes whether to prioritise my ethical accountability to the transformation of field or my ethical accountability to the review board. When our ethical dilemma requires us to choose between what the review board is mandating of us and what the ethnographic site needs of us, we have a reached an unsustainable situation which, in my view, will result in a further splitting-off of relevancy and relationship across the different spheres. I am not working so hard ethnographically only to be forced by the procedures of an ethical review board to walk away from bullying in the field in the name of protecting participants. Which participants? For whose benefit? Are there more basic ethical ideals regarding social transformation that might traverse the different spheres? If such ideals were taken up by review boards would the over-technocratisation stifle them in the end? How can review board power be contained so that it does not contaminate and restrict the potential for liberatory efforts which are themselves anchored in lives of those with whom we doing ethnographic research?

Futures and possibilities

Almost all of the chapters in the book indicated futures and possibilities. These futures/possibilities find their place in the dialogic conception of ethics. In this section of the chapter, we are called to imagine the possibilities, to imagine something ideal and to think concretely about how to be part of those futures/ possibilities. I present three domains of possibility, all of which position ethnographers as valued participants in ethical conversations:

1   education as dialogic opportunity
2   different as different
3   self-care in-between

Education as dialogic opportunity

According to Freire (1997/1970), education that does not reproduce the status quo demands dialogue – a dialogue across power and status relations, engaging perspectives across differences. Fox and Mitchell (Chapter 8, this volume) explicate just such a dialogue, drawing on several different sources with an educative goal in mind. With this explicit example, we can begin to imagine what it might look like to foster educative opportunities within and across the spheres through dialogue.

Traianou (Chapter 2, this volume) explicitly calls for ethnographers to enter a conversation with review board members about *phrónēsis* and how the everyday ethics of ethnography might be better understood through that concept. Such a dialogic opportunity could be taken up as part of an effort to educate review board members with respect to the difference between proceduralist and everyday ethics.

Review board members can be educated to take into account the various needs of ethnographers in the field. However, doing this would not really account for the legal anxieties that the board is managing on behalf of the institution. Perhaps these legal fears could be made more explicit and ethnographers could be better equipped to assuage those fears through the documentation that is provided (Chapter 3, this volume). It is difficult to address a problem when that problem is masquerading as a different problem – namely the protection of human (particularly vulnerable) subjects (Chapter 3, this volume). Dialogues that were able to point out this masquerading could free review board members from the silenced values of their work.

Additionally, in the education of our future ethnographers, there needs to be careful educational opportunities related to field ethics. Such opportunities would not be in the position of teaching ethnographers what is the right thing to do, but rather preparing scholars to be able to make ethical decisions in their fieldwork – including how those decisions might link with their theoretical orientations (Chapter 1, this volume) and sustained reflective practices (Chapter 8, this volume). Smette (Chapter 4, this volume) shared the intimate details of her consent-seeking and her work with partially participating groups. Such details are unfortunately unusual in publications, which might mean that our ethnography students do not have access to such intimate information. Moreover, we should see the dialogue of education an opportunity to develop the ethical capacities of our students. This is not merely a skill, but also an understanding of what is good in situ (Traianou, Chapter 2, this volume).

Last, ethnographers need to develop skills related to facilitating ethical conversations, but they also need to be able to foster this skill development in others. Our ethical dialogues need skilled participation. For review boards this is a technocratised skill, but with our participants this involves consciousness-raising, position-taking, listening and orienting towards understanding. We see how this breaks down in the story Dovemark shares with us. I argued that ethical decision-making in the field should be collectively engaged (similar to Busher's argument in Chapter 5 of this volume), but this collective conversation will work better with shared skills.

Different as different

It might be possible to locate the varying different ethical conversations relevant to a particular study. If this can be done, and one can refrain from judging one conversation based on the characteristics of another, then ethnographers might be able to appreciate each and prepare to actively engage in each. By recognising the differences in dialogue across the spheres, ethnographers would be better positioned to engage fruitfully across and within those distinct spheres. Smette argued (Chapter 4) that it was unproductive and unnecessary to locate the proceduralist ethics (which I have situated in the sphere of "review board dialogues") in opposition to everyday ethics (which would be part of the ethnographic field sphere). She proposed more of a continual relation which speaks to this idea of thinking of these conversations as different in the contrastive not oppositional sense.

Given the characteristics of the review board dialogue, perhaps it would be helpful to make the legal anxiety more explicit, while also bringing ethnographers into that conversation in a more meaningful way so that ethnographers could think about the legal aspects of their fieldwork. For example, the regulations requiring informed consent, when ethnography clearly does not function in the same limited way. Nevertheless, overarching consent might be accepted by ethnographers as meaningful from a legalistic perspective, though not as a replacement for (nor as a misleading representation of) an ongoing conversation about consent as part of the ethnographic process.

The kind of ethical guidance an ethnographer might need as she confronts ethical dilemmas and makes ethical decisions in the field cannot be obtained from a purely technocratic or strategic orientation. This kind of guidance is better when from other ethnographers, practitioners and perhaps participants.

In-between, ethnographers will want opportunities to reflect on and transform their own ethical decision-making. Drawing on self-knowledge, theoretical perspectives and trusted others, the dialogue of this sphere can involve a transformation of self-positioning in relation to review boards and ethnographic sites.

Traianou (Chapter 2) argued that *phrónēsis* would provide a better guide for ethnographic ethics than contemporary review boards with their proceduralist orientation. Traianou suggests that such proceduralism is antithetical to ethnographic ethics. Traianou recommends that perhaps review board members could be drawn into meaningful conversation with ethnographers regarding ethics, perhaps using *phrónēsis* as a guide for that conversation. It seems to me that such a conversation could help to clarify the difference that makes a difference without needing to morph the character of one sphere into the other.

Self-care in-between

One under-discussed topic in ethnographic ethics is self-care. Several chapters in this text allude to the implicit needs of ethnographers to be mindful and cared for with respect to their ethical work. These chapters indicate the intimacy of ethical work. In my own experience, as the lead in a long-term, team-based ethnography in a town we called Unityville, we were stretched thin emotionally and ethically – constantly choosing our battles when there was a lot at stake. I have written on these experiences before (Dennis 2009), but what I want to point out here is that our team met with a counsellor on Sunday afternoons in order to be able to deal with our own responses to the kinds of things we witnessed in the field and the ways those various activities, like bullying, positioned us as ourselves in the field, not as ethnographers, as if being ethnographers meant not being ourselves. Both Dovemark (Chapter 7) and Nikkanen (Chapter 6), in different ways, foreground this idea of being one's self in the field and centering one's ethical decisions through that ethical self-identity. We must have dialogic ways of doing this because we also know that despite our best intentions, we are not always ethically and morally correct. We also know that there are times when we do not understand the situation well enough to know how to act ethically. Thus, we cannot entirely depend upon the self for the kind of care is needs in-between in order to engage ethically in either sphere, but especially the demanding sphere of the ethnographic field site. As the ethnographic field sphere of dialogue runs away from the review board sphere of dialogue, the tension across the two will be unbearable for ethnographers in this in-between sphere.

Dovemark's consternation arose when she found herself betraying her own ethical commitments in the service of participants' reactions (most particularly calling her a liar). How was she to take care of herself in-between so that she could re-form her ethical decision-making in light of longstanding critical values and commitments? There is a reflective dialogue that involves the values one brings into the field along with one's sense of identity. This dialogue is itself productive of one's own identity. What Dovemark wrestled with is "who am I in this?" and "how can I live with what I do or not do?" Dovemark points out that if she is to judge her own behaviour in ethical terms (and not merely accept the judgement of others), she must "face dilemmas" concerning her own ontological identity and moral philosophy. This is self-care in-between the work of the field and the ethical wellbeing of the ethnographer.

Both Busher (Chapter 5) and Fox and Mitchell (Chapter 8) exemplify the ideals of such self-care dialogues as reflection and critical awareness about even the most easily taken-for-granted aspects of our ethnographic endeavors – like who is vulnerable and needs protecting. Authors seem to be suggesting that ethical reflection is important to self-care and to living out our ethnographic practices in ways that are ethically adequately for our own wellbeing and for the wellbeing of others, never assuming these are monolithic. This book overall is also an example of this kind of self-care through which ethnographers can share their experiences and ideas with others who care about being ethical in their practice.

Conclusion

The main point of this final chapter of the book is to locate the dialogic structure of ethical decision-making that allows us to imagine who we are as ethnographers in these dialogues. Doing so helps us to situate our sense of agency in conversation, and agency is always implicated in our understand of ethics. This is born out most obviously in the fact that ethnographers are finding more salient ethical decision-making in the field and in-between than in the procedural demands of review boards. Because ethics are imminently practical (Dennis 2018), if the technocratised proceduralism of review board practices split off more and more from the sphere of ethnographic fields, they might find themselves not actually engaged in ethics at all, instead serving as institutional bureaucrats divorced from even the spirit of the legal conversation. Ethnographers often find themselves in-between the spheres of these two conversations. Understanding that space as a contested and reflective dialogue will enable to ethical decision-making and ethical practices of our research work.

References

Barad, K. 2008. "Queer causation and the ethics of mattering". In *Queering the Non/Human*, edited by N. Giffney and M. Hird, 311–388. Farnham: Ashgate.

Dennis, B. 2009. "What does it mean when an ethnographer intervenes?" *Ethnography and Education* 4(2): 131–146.

Dennis, B. 2010. "Ethical dilemmas in the field: The complex nature of doing education ethnography". *Ethnography and Education* 5(2): 123–127.

Dennis, B. 2018. "Working without/against a compass: Ethical dilemmas in educational ethnography". In *Handbook on Ethnography of Education*, edited by D. Beach, C. Bagley and S. Marques da Silva, 51–70. Hoboken, NJ: Wiley Press.

Freire, P. 1997/1970. *Pedagogy of the Oppressed*. Harmondsworth: Penguin.

Habermas, J. 1998. *Between Facts and Norms: Contributions to a Discourse Theory of Law and Democracy*, trans. W. Rehg. Boston, MA: MIT Press. Reprint edition.

Kitchener, K.S. and Kitchener, R.F. 2009. "Social science research ethics: Historical and philosophical issues". In *The Handbook of Social Research Ethics*, edited by D.M. Mertens and P.E. Ginsberg, 5–22. New York: Sage.

Lather, P. 2009. "Issues of validity in openly ideological research: Between and rock and a soft place". In *Turning Points in Qualitative Research: Tying Knots in a Handkerchief*, edited by Y. Lincoln and N. Denzin, 185–216. Walnut Creek, CA: Altamira Press.

Index

Page numbers in *italics* refer to figures. Page numbers in **bold** refer to tables.